# THE NIGHT THEY BLITZED THE RITZ

## The Ritz

*Memoirs of a Bomb-Alley Kid*

## John Bull

Published by
Channel Island Publishing
Unit 3b, Barette Commercial Centre
La Route du Mont Mado
St John, Jersey JE3 4DS

ISBN 978-1-905095-25-2

Printed by Cromwell Press, Trowbridge, Wiltshire

# Acknowledgements

The nicest thing about writing these memoirs is that I met many other survivors of the Luftwaffe's war on Gosport and shared memories of those times with them.

I'm particularly indebted to my cousins Peter and Brenda Wolland, Winston and Judy Wolland, and Freda and Les Baker. Peter particularly for always being there, in times happy or sad, and lately for his amazing memory of how the old town of Gosport — now vanished — looked and felt back then.

Thanks to Peter Greenaway for the picture of his redoubtable centenarian mother, Ivy, and her remarkable story; my boyhood chums Tom and Robin Fayers; noted archive mole Richard Watts; photographer Patrick Miller; Gosport's 'Mr Information' Ian Jeffrey; Gosport Museum curator Oonagh Palmer; Gosport Borough Council's Catherine MacDonald; Debbie Croker of the The News, Portsmouth; local historian Ron Brown; and the priceless expertise of Chief Petty Officer (GI) Alf Batley (RN retired) in checking the finer details of my navy 'dits.' I am also grateful to Tim Hughes, director of the International Bar Association based in Auckland NZ, for the story and picture of George Bizos and the HMS Kimberley rescue.

Most of the original photographs, including family pictures, were taken by one or other of the Lawrences, and I must thank Tony Lawrence and the family for kindly allowing me carte blanche to reproduce them. The charming picture of the steam ferries and the photograph of the Avenue Road bomb damage are from the Gosport Museum collection.

My gratitude also to my wife Amanda Field for her unflagging encouragement and her professional assistance in editing the text.

Most of the book was written during my long winter breaks over two years at The Imperial Hotel, Sliema, Malta — where the staff's companionable care and attention made the whole job go so much more smoothly.

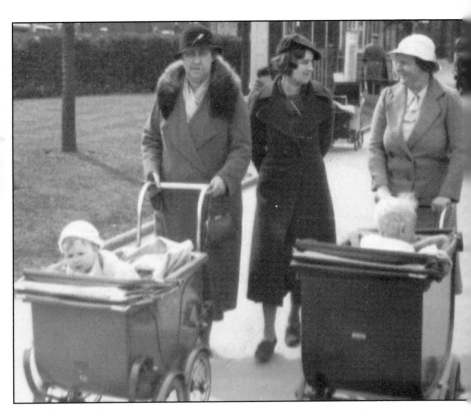

Going over the water....I'm the forward-looking one in the pram that
Grannie is pushing, while my mother Nell chats to a fellow ferry traveller

# Introduction
## Going over the Water

O ne day Gosport folk may be able to ride across to Portsmouth through a tunnel under the harbour. No longer will ferry passengers be exposed to rude blasts of gale-driven rain, or have to seek shelter below instead of taking the air on deck. In short, no fun at all.

The dream isn't anything new. It's been a long time coming. When I was at school, I recall seeing at the public library a model for a proposed Gosport-Portsmouth tunnel: this was just after World War II and, I gather, it had been around a while then. It was the fanciful Kearney tube.

The design was very much of the Thirties, with lots of functional concrete and glass, hauntingly Art Deco in green and blue like the Piccadilly Line. In the model they used a glass tube to represent the tunnel that went under the harbour. The waves were made of Plasticine, I think, and such a rare shade of blue-green that whenever I have noticed that colour since, I'm instantly reminded of the tunnel.

I was desperate to ride in it and badgered everyone who might know when it would happen. But over the years the dream faded, as familiarity with marvels like flying the Atlantic to New York led to a loss of wonder and a certain disillusion because such things never do live up to their promise. We're so intent on grabbing the future that we fail to realise that flying to New York loses its edge when everyone else can do it too, and it isn't the future any more.

The past is more reliable. It tends to retain its magic; indeed, thanks to nostalgia, the magic seems to grow with the years. That's how it is for me anyway and the purpose of this set of memoirs is hopefully to entertain anyone who feels the same.

A trip from Gosport to Pompey when I was small was called Going over the Water. My mother would pop round to my Grannie's and say: "I've got to buy a new skirt: shall we go over the water?" Then I'd be bundled into layers of clothing against the cold, strapped into my pushchair and skilfully woman-handled onto the heaving deck of the ferry Venus.

Those old ferries were the perfect symbol of life in Gosport. Overall about 60 ft, they lay comparatively low in the water with a sharp bow, a railed foredeck with a chain across the gangway, and a step up to the maindeck with a three-sided box containing a disproportionately large wheel for the skipper at the helm. Immediately behind was a tall, slender funnel in cream with a black band around the top, like the tip on a cigarette. A row of seats each side met in a curve round the graceful stern. There was also a midships range of seats built around a skylight above the engine room and after-cabin below. Access to the fore and aft cabins was by a gangway at the side of the foredeck, with a similar one at the stern.

Along both sides of the ferry lifebelts hung like the shields on a Viking longboat, which gave the little vessels their distinctive, picture-postcard look.

That jolly little boat, punching the tide in a fresh breeze, was just made for little boys like me. The sting of salt spray as she plunged into a wave, the scream of a gull swooping into the thin stream of black smoke from her funnel, the sights and sounds of a busy, busy harbour....with little steam pinnaces, agleam with brightwork, darting from ship to shore, the great warships at anchor or — wonder of wonders — a lean destroyer slipping out past the Sally Port with sailors 'just like Daddy,' in their blue uniforms, stiffly lining the foredeck.

Picture a typical journey just before World War II:

In a flurry of churning water, the Venus heaves away from the floating pontoon and heads northabout along the Gosport shore, past the constant hammering from Camper and Nicholson's ship and yacht-builders' yard, opening up glimpses of Royal Clarence Yard, the navy's historic victualling stores (dating from Georgian days with elegant architecture to match), the naval ordnance depot at Priddy's Hard, the Hardway shore in Fareham Creek and, as she puts about to head eastwards, a fine view of Portchester Castle (founded by the Romans) with the green Portsdown hill behind.

Nearing the Pompey side the ferry sweeps inwards past the dockyard signal tower and the oil fuel jetty with, on a good day, a battleship such as HMS Hood alongside. There's a long view of the sunlit waterfront on Portsmouth Hard and its half-a-dozen pubs, among them the Half Moon, the Ship Anson, and the Keppel's Head; and then a churning backwatering as she hauls alongside the Pompey pontoon, under the dark, barnacle-encrusted piles of the Southern Railway's harbour station and cheekily lines up beneath the bows of one of the grander Southern Railway paddle steamers for the Isle of Wight.

All this in the time it takes to boil an egg.

Returning southabout, the Venus backs out to clear the sharp bow of the island ferry Merstone, with her two great, unwieldy paddle wheels mounted amidships. And then she runs down the narrow water: to port are the piles under the harbour station, and to starboard, just clear of the fairway, lie two black-dirty fleet coalers left over from the days when all ships burned coal, long anchored, neglected. Down towards the gunwharf and HMS Vernon, past the mercantile docks of the Camber, turning west so that you see Spithead and the distant Isle of Wight framed by the narrow harbour mouth, only 200 feet wide; and then past Blockhouse, and Haslar creek where submarines nest like surfaced sharks. Just before landing on the Gosport pontoon, the ferry passes two old 'wooden walls' — Foudroyant, formerly the frigate HMS Trincomalee, and Implacable, originally a French man o'war named after the Breton admiral Douguay-Trouin (they scuttled her in the late Forties off the back of the Wight. And I'm glad to say it took the gunners of a modern warship all day to sink her. Lucky for them she wasn't firing back).

Against the usual way of things, the ferry kept its romance as I got older. I used to stand in the gangway and watch the oil-burning engines below. They were real then, gleaming copper and brass, pistons moving, cranks and shafts turning, the engineer opening and closing hot valves with a piece of cotton waste in his hand. They were proper engines: you can see ones like them in a museum, but you can't smell the hot oil, hear the hiss of steam, or feel the power vibrating the steel plates under your feet.

Below, the cabin was a snug, even romantic place to be, say coming home from the pictures in Pompey on a cold night. Shadows were deep in the dim cabin light. Those two over there, faces half-lit by the glow of a cigarette, could they be Peter Lorre and Sidney

Greenstreet? What are they plotting? Have they found a new clue to Dashiel Hammett's lost Maltese Falcon, or unmasked Eric Ambler's Dimitrios Makropoulis?

On a mild night you could stand on deck and watch the lights of Gosport heave nearer, the breeze fresh in your face. Ah, the girls I've cuddled in the dark of the stern seats, under a sky full of stars, back and forth, a romantic cruise that lasted until the skipper gruffly ordered me to "take the young med home before yer git into trouble."

The old rival chain ferry from Gosport Hard, which we affectionately called the floating bridge, was even more romantic since it took you straight to the heart of picturesque Old Portsmouth with its classic Georgian houses, narrow alleys and artful taverns, echoing with memories of Nelson and his band of brothers; the elite high-flying upper yardsmen, the cream of man o'war crews; the Royal Marines; the press gang; and the tarts. The floating bridge ran for the last time in the late Fifties forcing cars to go the boring, long way round, some 20 miles or so.

However, a motorbike you could take on board the passenger ferry with you. In my teens I found it a struggle getting my bike on and off if the water was choppy, and I remember one of the mates, who had been at school with me, sneering: "You're a bloody good hand at sitting on them," as his strong arms heaved the bike on to the pontoon. Fair comment.

He probably thought my lot was better than his. But those ferry crews — skipper, mate and engineer — I used to envy them. I might, I suppose, have gone mad with boredom, but that's the point you see, we never appreciate that. All we see is the comforting routine, the same trip, over and over and over again, a ritual life. With a break now and again for tea and tobacco. You must admit it has its attractions.

To confess: I still nip down for a bracing trip on the ferry every now and again. Especially on days when I'm feeling a bit blue and need cheering up. And I suppose I'll try out the tunnel, if I live long enough. But only once.

To put it another way: My first day at work was New Year's Day 1953. I took the ferry to Pompey, which all my life had been 1d, and found it had gone up to three ha'pence. A warning that my time of innocence was over.

All aboard for Pompey....steam-launch ferries pictured Gosportside

# Chapter One
## The Secret Life of a Bookie's Runner

Before I was old enough to go to school, in the summer of 1939, my grandfather Alfred Ferré would often call to take me for a walk in the morning. He'd sweep me up in his arms and I would reach out to pull at the ends of his neat, brown moustache and run my fingers up and down the stubble on his cheek.

"Don't go getting him into trouble, Dad," my mother said, mysteriously. What trouble could I possibly get into with Grandpa? They both laughed as if it was a shared joke.

Our walk took us to parts of old Gosport around Clarence Square, its faded Georgian houses framed by the blue-green waters of Portsmouth harbour, with the fresh morning sky above reflected in dozens of rain puddles across the roadway, a scene untouched by the streamlined 1930s. The first call was to Sam Wolland's barber shop in King Street. I was placed on a bench seat in the window, where I could stare at a line of whiskered, older gentlemen, all dark waistcoats and silver watchchains, sitting at their ease, sending up a blue fug of pipe smoke and reading newspapers.

"You're next, Guv'nor," said Sam to Grandpa, deferentially, nodding to one of the deep leather chairs with high foot-rails and adjustable neck-rests. Sam's brother had married Grandpa's elder daughter Gert, so respect was due. Grandpa was practically lying down in the chair as the lather boy, mug and badger brush in hand, worked up a soapy foam over his face.

Meanwhile Sam took one of the bright razors and stropped it on a long piece of leather fixed to the wall. Then with delicate speed, using long strokes of the naked blade, he shaved Grandpa's cheeks so close that they shone. The boy then took a shoe brush and cloth and gave Grandpa's black boots a high polish before he got down from the chair, where he stood rubbing a hand over his face with great satisfaction.

Grandpa spoke to all the men, and most of them slipped little packages into his hand, which he transferred deftly to the pockets of his dark suit. I knew what that was about. My grandfather was a bookie's runner. These were the betting slips, wrapped around the stake money for their fancies in that day's racing. It was against the law, of course.

In the days before betting shops took much of the excitement out of a flutter on the horses, you could only legally bet at the course, or if you had an account with a bookie or 'turf accountant' as the posher ones called themselves. There were a couple of these in Gosport High Street, small offices with discreet gold lettering on the door, one I think next to the Swiss Café, the only 'foreign' restaurant we used to have in those days and so respectable it was the regular meeting place of Gosport Rotary Club.

My dark-haired, dark-eyed grandfather winked at me, put his finger to his lips, and led me out into the street. To call him a bookie's, or any other kind of runner, was part of the joke. His feet were so bad from years of ill-fitting boots he had trouble keeping up with me.

So we crept along to the ferry gardens, amid the fresh, unforgettable scent of a thousand wallflowers, a sort of leitmotif for our breezy waterfront town, where he sat on his usual bench, lit his pipe, and waited for business. Housewives, shop girls, passing sailors, all manner of people stopped for a chat, a quick look round for the bobby, and then the underhand passing of the slip.

After a while we walked slowly up the High Street and into Stoke Road, to a pub called the No Place Tavern, and into the snug, all fumed oak and spotless polished glass, where Grandpa sat under a sign that said 'No betting on these Premises.' According to the law I wasn't even supposed to go in there but he sat me up on the bar for my treat, a glass of lemonade, still lemonade, not the gassy stuff. Grandpa, the ringleader in all this law-breaking, took half a pint of old and mild. Naturally I had to have a sip; strong it was, which bound us even closer in crime. If my mother had known!

Here in the snug the talk was of horses with strange names like Moonraker and Mother's Ruin. Jockeys like the young, but up-and-coming Gordon Richards. Phrases like 'bottom weight of a field of 3-year-olds,' or 'nowhere last time out' or 'odds-on favourite' could be heard. Grandpa often advised against backing a horse each-way; that is dividing the stake half for a win and half for a place in the first three.

"You must show the horse you've got confidence in him," he'd say. A raised forefinger and an intelligent look: "They know, you know."

All his clients used to sign their slips with code names, such as 'Lucky Seven', 'The Grasshopper' or 'Mother Brown.' My father, when home from sea, called himself 'Shanghai.' Grandpa knew all these code names by heart. He himself operated under the highly secret name of 'Packet,' the best bookie's runner in Gosport.

By the time we left the No Place, Grandpa was clinking audibly with the cash in his pockets. It was clearly a big race day, and there might have been as much as a fiver on him, more than a fortnight's pay for a skilled tradesman, all in sixpences and shillings. A half-crown bet was a wild plunge in that place, in those days.

This was not the time to bump into a policeman. So we took a detour through the vast green space of Walpole Park, strolling round the cockle pond while keeping a sharp lookout. Then a hurried dive into a house in Willis Road, alongside the park. Out again in seconds. This was a 'safe' house where the runners paid in, and the bets were timed by a trusted bookie's clerk, who also collected the cash and brought the winnings back later.

That evening, while sadly I was in bed, Grandpa would slip back to Willis Road, collect his share of winnings and set off on his evening round of the local pubs paying out the lucky ones. On top of his commission from the bookie, everyone who had a decent win was expected to give him the price of a drink.

Now and again the police would swoop, haul everyone into court, and they'd all be fined five shillings and get their names listed in very small print, in the Portsmouth Evening News. The bookie, of course, reimbursed them all, regarding it as a hazard of the trade. The safe house would move, temporarily, somewhere else and they'd all start again.

Actually my Grandpa, alias the elusive Packet, was never caught. And born criminal as I was, I was rather pleased about that.

Man in the shadows....the camera (nearly) captures the elusive
Packet on a trip to Cheddar Caves with his wife Harriet and son
Bill, no doubt on the proceeds of a betting coup. Note the
inquisitive copper in the background

# Chapter Two
# On the Gosport Riviera

I remember a Sunday trip to the seashore at Stokes Bay with my parents, grandparents, uncles, aunt and cousins, probably because it was typical of what we did as a family, as indeed did most Gosport families, but more likely because it was the last one we had — towards the end of the summer of 1939 — before the beach was sealed off by barbed wire and concrete tank traps against the threat of invasion, and the sea sown with mines; big black-steel globes with horns on that were said to need only one nudge to blow an enemy ship in half.

Stokes Bay: my uncles called it the Gosport Riviera. One-time part of the moated fortifications that protected Gosport on the seaward side and, in 1939, a borough council dream of a seaside resort which ran to a half-mile crescent of dirty, oily shingle, a concrete promenade and a shabby beach cafe.

Oh and slightly inland, set back on the road, the latest attraction — the Penny Palace, a magnificent Art Deco toilet block in curving red brick surrounded by neat lawns and shrubs, and boasting inside a range of urinals, cubicles and washbasins, spotless in gleaming porcelain, the surrounds tiled to shame a Roman villa, and all calculated to draw gasps of envy from out-of-town visitors whose own town hall could not run to opulence like it.

Above each washbasin was a looking glass etched with decorations so achingly Thirties that to picture it now makes my eyes brim with tears of nostalgia. Last time I saw it standing, the Penny Palace was boarded up, shamefacedly trying to hide itself behind an unkempt hedge, like a forgotten actress hiding at home and turning all her mirrors to the wall. With its gorgeous interior gutted long ago, it seemed to recognise itself as an embarrassment to the superior, go-ahead plastic, disposable Gosport of the twenty-first century acknowledging with a sigh that its days were numbered.

What is equally sure is that now that the perennially unlucky town council have bulldozed it (in, it must be said, a sneaky early morning operation to avoid protests), having learned absolutely nothing from the destruction by earlier councils of Gosport's wonderful Thirties open-air swimming pool and the Art Deco masterpiece of Lee Tower, they will suddenly discover that the rest of the world actually treasures such glories and will pay good money to come and admire them. "Too late, too late," I hear again that familiar cry....

But back to the family. We'd go out to the bay on a green double-decker, open-top bus, courtesy of the Provincial bus company. It used to set us down just around the corner from the Palace and here the party divided; men and boys strolling back into Alverstoke village and the pub, the Sir Charles Napier (named for a barely remembered, old Victorian general doubtless known to his men as Black Charlie) while women and girls marched off to grab the best picnic spot on the grass as near as possible to the beach.

The Napier was different because it had a room where kids were allowed. We were supposed to sit — in silence — on the long, bent-cane furniture that ran round three walls. The other wall held the dartboard and a serving hatch into the bar. According to the pecking order, we kids swapped sly digs and punches in a sort of soundless struggle. I never minded this vow of silence as it allowed me to concentrate on the adult conversation, pretty much my favourite pastime.

My father and uncles treated the landlord and landlady with marked respect, as they did anyone of my Grandpa's generation. Such older men were deferred to, listened to, offered cigarettes or a pinch of baccy, and were not expected to pay for their own drink. Nobody mentioned the coming war. What was there to say? Its inevitability was an accepted fact. These were people who had fought one 'war to end all wars' already or, like my dad, as professionals were going to be the first into action at sea.

I was treated to a glass of still lemonade (not the gassy stuff) and a packet of crisps. The men lit up Woodbines and drank mild ale from straight, no-nonsense glasses. When my father picked up his drink, the entire pint glass disappeared in his sailor's fist.

Uncle Jim might kick off with a remark or two about Pompey who back in the spring had won the FA Cup, beating Wolves at Wembley 4-1.

"Din't you used to play?" the landlord politely asked. Jim nodded, looking suitably embarrassed-but-pleased.

"Oh, that was years ago," he said. The conversation widened to a discussion of the club's chances in the coming season. The one that never happened. And Pompey kept the FA Cup for a record six years, a fact that became a standard sports question in pub quizzes.

Football managers also lasted longer in those days and Jack Tinn led Portsmouth FC in some style for about 20 years — though many thought his tendency to wear spats, the uniform of the upper class twit as played by musical comedy favourite Claude Dampier, lowered Pompey's tough reputation and disguised Jack's brilliance. He left them off once and Pompey went down 0-2 (to Bolton Wanderers I think) and that started the legend of the lucky spats that Jack never again left at home on a Saturday. He was definitely wearing them at Wembley in 1939.

To this day Pompey's supporters worldwide still regard that as the club's finest hour. (As I write this Pompey have a date in a couple of weeks time to play Cardiff City at Wembley — for the FA Cup. I'm sticking my neck out and forecasting a win).

\*\*\*\*\*\*\*\*\*\*

Mum with her brothers Bill (centre) and Alf (right) with Bill's dog Pom

Gosport families each had their favourite Sunday pitch at the bay, on the pebbly beach, on the grassy bits among the gorse bushes, or on the banks of the moat that ran across the backland. Everyone had something to carry; towels, a blanket, sandwiches or a pork pie, the cricket bat, maybe a primus stove, or wood for a fire to make tea and, of course, the kettle.

Our lot favoured a lone spit of sand among the pebbles close to the high-water mark. The women and girls had already grabbed the spot and laid out blankets and towels to show possession. Peter and I, as the younger boys, were sent to gather a few twigs and bits of dry driftwood for a fire.

Sometimes the little grassy dell amid the shingle that the family had favoured for generations was already occupied, so then would begin the tricky process of 'finding-the-best-spot,' starting with a quasi-democratic discussion among the adults about where else to sit, all standing around clutching bundles with aching arms, and vastly entertaining other families already in place. It ended when Grannie dropped in her tracks and defied anyone to move her.

That settled, the kids would tear off their clothes and rush screaming into the sea. The adults reclined on the shingle looking up from a newspaper or book every few minutes to tell each other "This is nice." "This is very nice." "Isn't this nice?"

A typical Sunday line-up in order of seniority would be Grandpa and Grandma, Uncle Alf, Uncle Bill, Auntie Gert and Uncle Jim, and my Mum and Dad — Ellen and John. Gert's children were Jimmy, Freda, Edna and Peter, and I was the baby of the family.

Despite the stiff breeze, a prevailing westerly and prevailingly chilly, the sea eventually had to be faced. The best word to describe that first encounter with the water is 'refreshing'. It's amazing how long the average British family can stay in the sea, splashing and playing with the children, the nicest part being when it stops and you can return, skin tingling from salt spray, to lie on the warm shingle.

The playing fields of Eton might well have produced the likes of Black Charlie Napier but, as we were about to find out, modern warfare called for an entire population of more stoical people, their character moulded no doubt by the British seaside holiday.

I recall Freda and Edna pulling me into the surf, where the green water boiled and frothed around me, then lifting me over the crest of a curling wave, before dumping me down again into the water that splashed up my nose and into my eyes, my mouth stinging from the taste of salt.

Later I'd be stretched out to dry on the patchy mix of sand and shingle. At my feet would be a small pile of seashells, found for me by the girls. Some were tiny and as delicate as fine porcelain, and lined with shining mother of pearl. Others were larger, rarer, shaped like half a lemon cut lengthwise with two rows of very fine, pointy teeth down the middle. If you held one to your ear you could hear a distant, lazy swish-swish of waves rolling onshore.

Nobody bothered with the shells of clams or oysters, or mussels or cockles, or winkles. Too ordinary. But there was another family of shells, up to an inch long, roundly conical, banded with pretty markings, no two exactly the same. These were often collected for a variety of uses notably, I was soon to discover, at the infant school where they were used to teach us to count.

From under a floppy hat to protect me from burning, I'd turn my head to watch the sunlight reflected in millions of brilliants dancing on the wavetops, a soft breeze fanning my cheek, until the sound of the waves became so soporific that the cries and laughter of the dozens of children around us faded into a faint lullaby that rose and fell on my ears until I drifted off to sleep....

Later: "Wake up Baby John. Here's some pop for you." This was Auntie Gert offering me a glass of Tizer cordial, sparkling in the sunlight just like the sparkle on the sea. It went down well, washing the salt from the mouth and giving me an immediate appetite for tea.

The picnic menu usually involved slices of polony or saveloy, or chunks of pork pie, and sandwiches: tomato or cucumber, cheese and pickle, and for the smaller kids, apple or banana sandwiches. There was always a big fruit cake to be sliced up and served with a cup of tea. Peter and I would be sent for the water. It meant carrying the kettle through the arid, dark-green, faintly plum-scented gorse bushes that scratched my legs and filled the air with specks of dried seeds that flew up as we brushed past and made us sneeze. We found a path that led up to a tall, iron standpipe set at the top of the bank alongside the moat.

It had a long chain dangling from the top to hold the tin cup so that people could get a drink. Halfway up the pipe was a big silver button that Peter pushed in while I held the kettle against the spout to catch the water. There was also a large shallow tray at the bottom that was always filled with spilled water so that people's dogs could have a drink, too.

Uncle Jim had a small fire of twigs going by the time we got back, and the kettle was soon singing away on its circle of big stones. The mothers made due ceremony out of making the tea: the pot had to be thoroughly warmed, the tea measured and spooned in, one for each cup and one more for the pot. It had to stand for exactly one minute and 30 seconds, and the milk, for those who wanted it, poured into a warmed cup first. Nearly everyone took sugar; some of the men preferred their tea black.

Uncle Bill wanted a slice of lemon in his and was told by Grannie that he should have remembered to bring a lemon himself — though, now she came to think of it, he was sour-faced enough already — and while he was about it he could also do a bit more of the carrying in future.

Ah, the future....what future? This was the last summer of peace.

These Sundays invariably ended with the family trailing back from the beach along The Avenue to the crossroads and The Wiltshire Lamb. There we all sat around a long table in the garden, under trees filtering the dazzle of the setting sun. Beers and shandies for the adults, and lemonade for the kids, to get the salt out of the throat.

Mostly we were too sated with fresh air and sunshine to do more than sit. I fancy I have always remembered that last Sunday evening with a lump in my throat, as if my tired family were savouring the moment, somehow aware that everything they had, the world they knew — imperfect, cruel-hard sometimes, but the life that they were used to — was about to disappear for ever.

I believe they could see it in the smoke curling up from Grandpa's pipe, in the long shadows cast by the sinking sun, and as my eyelids droop I seem to hear the lingering, faltering birdsong in the trees, never quite ending, just wistfully fading away.

And how come I remember so much of these days at the beach anyway? Easy. Whenever Peter and I were billeted together overnight during the tough times of the war, especially at Christmas, we would re-run our memories of these long lost, idyllic days. And as new babies came along, we passed on this traditional folklore of that magic time that ended in 1939.

"Tell us about Before-the-War, Peter."

"All right then. Well, me and John and all the family used to go every Sunday to Stokes Bay...."

Grandpa pictured in happier times with pals at the Queen's Hotel

# Chapter Three
# A Cross between Carmen and Cleopatra

Before the war began and my father went away to sea, my parents rented a house in Avenue Road, an Edwardian bay-and-forecourt terrace a stone's throw from the tall, white gates of the goods yard entrance to Gosport railway station and the Southern Railway line between Gosport and Fareham.

The sound of shunting steam engines pushing and pulling wagons, the clanking and rolling of iron wheels on rails and the knock-on beat of clanging buffers was an underlying accompaniment to life in these streets, as was the coming and going of coal merchants' carts and other traffic, mostly horse-drawn.

People would only have noticed the noise if for some reason it stopped. It fitted well with the other daily noises that made up the background music to life in Gosport in 1939. There was the daily rattle of small-arms fire from the Browndown rifle ranges and, closer to home, the practice shooting from the army barracks between us and the town centre. Overhead was the occasional drone of a biplane, probably the noble swordfish, known to the bold flyers of the Fleet Air Arm as 'the old stringbag.' These were accepted by everyone as simple, everyday things....but they cast a long shadow.

As the Thirties poet Louis MacNeice wrote in his evocative Autumn Journal:

"The spinster picking up stitches
Not raising her eyes to the planes that pass
Northward from Lee-on-Solent."

The railway line ran only from Gosport to Fareham, five miles up the Gosport peninsula to the north west, though there had been a branch spur to Stokes Bay and Lee-on-the-Solent, sadly shut down only few years before. I could just about recall as a toddler, aged about two, the little green engine puffing past the back garden of our earlier house at 100 King's Road, which backed onto that section of line, then used only for shunting.

The goods yard was a kind of small-scale marshalling yard and busier than the traffic along the line merited, which was mostly coal in high-sided open trucks, because it was linked to the naval and military railway that ran from Gosport station eastwards to the victualling and ordnance yards of the Royal Navy, alongside Portsmouth harbour.

For this reason, the area was a likely target for German bombers and in fact the station was an early casualty of the Blitz. It has remained a romantic ruin ever after. Pity, because it was a palatial Victorian structure, much higher and more imposing than Gosport had any right to; tall and spacious, with Doric columns, a glass roof and high glazed windows finished in the beloved Victorian colours of cream and beige. The imperious Victoria had her own elegant apartment, a kind of Royal Room-in-Waiting.

The station was built so that Her Majesty could avoid going to Portsmouth on her way to her holiday home, Osborne House, on the Isle of Wight. She preferred to come to Gosport via the line from London which passed through Alton and Fareham, later called the Meon Valley line. She'd arrive at her magnificent station in Spring Garden Lane, Gosport, and then take a carriage to Royal Clarence Yard, the victualling depot, where she joined the Royal Yacht Victoria and Albert to cross the Solent.

The accepted story was that Her Majesty had fallen out with the citizens of Portsmouth because she claimed that they were rude to her consort, her saintly Prince Albert. They did not pay him sufficient due as husband of the Queen Empress. In fact the whole sorry situation was a total misunderstanding which came about purely because of a misprint in the Portsmouth Evening News. In an early report of the royal couple arriving by train at Portsmouth to embark on the yacht, the paper announced: "The Portsmouth populace cheered as Queen Victoria pissed over the bridge...."

Or so my grandfather, who claimed to have read the article himself, happily told everyone. This was, of course, materially impossible by at least 30 years, but nobody ever felt like challenging him about it. It was just too good a story.

It was one-up to Gosport in its constant rivalry with her big sister Pompey, home of the Royal Navy, that the queen preferred to join her yacht at Gosport and consequently the town had this magnificent station with a large spanning roof and colonnades with pillars of Old Testament dimension that I mentally linked with Sunday School descriptions of the temple of Solomon. I would not be surprised to learn that Cecil B de Mille was inspired to base his design for the House of the Philistines in his epic Samson and Delilah on Gosport station.

My mother, Ellen (Nell to family and close friends), was the giver of my life and the most important thing in it. In that she never had any competition from my mostly absent father, though there were times in my childhood when, successively, my Grannie, Grandpa, Auntie Gert, Cousin Freda and Uncle Alf, did take precedence on my hero list.

In the Avenue Road days my mother's Number One slot was threatened only by the latest sensation for kids: the Beano, and later the Dandy, and anything at all to do with cowboys (in which category I generously included Canada's Royal North West Mounted Police or Mounties).

I conjure up a picture of a slender woman just south of 30 with light hair, English complexion, pretty rather than beautiful, in a flattering modern frock, with long skirt and high heels. She was lucky to live at a time when the chain stores could offer inexpensive clothes based on some of the greatest designer styles of the twentieth century. We're talking Schiaparelli here, or Molyneux, as worn by Claudette Colbert, Bette Davis, Barbara Stanwyck, Joan Crawford, Myrna Loy and the young Marlene Dietrich.

My mother had a high-arch Roman nose, and believe me, she could put on an arrogant, imposing hauteur if she felt slighted in any way. And if that failed she would resort to gypsy methods and issue a pagan, resounding and fearsome curse on the offender. Imagine a cross between Carmen and Cleopatra. She had a husky singing voice, a sort of deep tremolo, really suited to the sadder torch songs of the time. I'd be playing on the floor with my clockwork train and I'd hear her sing:

"My Yiddisher momma, I miss her more than ever now. Her jewels and her treasures, she found them in her baby's smile...."

And the family all agreed she could jerk a tear out of you better than Sophie Tucker, the cave-mouthed Yankee chanteuse who made the song famous.

This temperament made Mum a difficult proposition for my father and her family who tended to walk on eggshells around her. The only person who seemed to be able to handle her successfully, to take the sting out of her so to speak, was my Grannie Harriet, known to her intimates as Allie. It's a fact that my mother never lived more than a couple of streets away from her mother until the old lady died, and after that it was really too late to shove off and start somewhere else.

The point about the fashion copies of the Thirties was not lost on my grandmother, who felt she had missed out. Born around 1880, she struggled all her life to throw off what she saw as the dull and deadly strait-jacket of Victorian values, a metaphor made manifest for her as she approached her sixties by the pinching of her corsets.

A shopping trip with these two just before World War II was a real education for me. It was also a foundation course of sorts, because I seem to have been steeped in this era, certainly it left me with a lifetime affection for Art Deco styles, the furniture of the Bauhaus, and jewellery by Tiffany.

For example, the first time I visited the city of Nice I arrived in a June rainstorm and took shelter in the grands magasins of the Avenue Victor Hugo. I had a distinct feeling of déjà vu. It persisted, and I puzzled over why I felt instantly at home in a Mediterranean city I'd never seen before. Even if that day it was dripping under the clouds more like Manchester than the full, hot light of the Midi, Nice was like nowhere I'd been. I was wandering from one department store to another, dodging showers.... and then the penny dropped. It was the shops themselves, of course. As a child on the eve of the war I was often in department stores almost identical to these — but that was in Commercial Road, Portsmouth, before the bombs tore the heart out of Pompey's shopping centre.

In Nice there had been no bombs; the great department stores were preserved just as I remembered their contemporaries in Portsmouth with their elegant, straight-cut stone facades, their grand windows and galleries decorated with polished wood and ironwork, floor on floor, linked by imposing lifts and sweeping staircases in the 'modern' idiom. Les Galleries Lafayettes, instead of Pompey's Landport Drapery Bazaar, Printemps instead of Melanies, and C et A instead of C and A. No wonder I always feel at home in these great palaces.

In contrast my father James, but always referred to as John, or Johnny Bull, was the invisible man. I do not recall him joining any of these shopping trips during my early childhood. Twice he appeared suddenly in my life. When I was born he was at the start of a two-and-a-half year commission to China, where, distinguished by a full set of whiskers, he served in the crew of a gunboat up the Yangtse river.

So my infant life changed abruptly with the homecoming of this dark stranger. Then, no sooner had I got used to the idea of him being around — tall, slender, deep-voiced and immensely strong — he vanished again, this time not to re-appear until I had grown from a toddler to a lippy, street urchin, a Bomb Alley Kid with most of my life prejudices already well-formed.

If that was a problem, it was one that I don't think either of us ever completely resolved. His service was a strange mystery to me in the early years of the war. How come he was never able to get home to see me? Other kids' fathers got home on leave, didn't they?

Mum: left in Carmen gypsy mode....................and right in Cleopatra style

Dad: left as a young sailor planning a fruit farm in South Africa and right with full set of whiskers – and some of the gunboat crew up the Yangtse river

His timing was never good. He was due to leave the navy when his 12-year engagement ran out and planned to join a shipmate who'd already emigrated to South Africa to grow oranges in the sun. Bill was doing all right with a fruit farm near Durban. But the calendar flipped over to September 1939.

Hitler had other ideas — he invaded Poland; the Luftwaffe bombed Warsaw; Neville Chamberlain declared war and my father and skilled professional sailors like him were 'invited' to stay on for the duration. Despite the mythology that has been bandied about since, Dad and his fellow matelots had no illusions about it being 'all over by Christmas.' For the Royal Navy the so-called 'phoney war' in 1939 and early 1940 never existed.

The war at sea began on the first day — September 3, 1939 — with the torpedoing of the liner Athenia by U-boat U30 off the northwest of Ireland while on passage to Montreal. The dead included nearly 100 women and children.

Only a fortnight later the aircraft carrier HMS Courageous was torpedoed by U-boat U29 in the Western Approaches of the Atlantic with the loss of 500 sailors, more than half her crew. This tragedy widowed many young naval wives in Gosport — among them Mrs Ivy Owen whose husband Bernard was a navy aircrewman, an observer, in the carrier. Four years before Ivy had proudly moved into the first house to be built in Gosport's Strathmore Road, part of the development of Admiral Field's estate. Now she was left to cope alone with her young son....and there were to be many more like her in the cruel war at sea.

However, just before Christmas Britain was cheered up by news from South America of the Battle of the River Plate in which three cruisers — Exeter, Ajax and Achilles — forced the scuttling of the German battleship Graf Spey at Montevideo.

Meanwhile my father was ordered to Scapa Flow, about as far from Pompey as it was possible to go and still be in Britain. And no doubt my mother missed him. But I sensed early on that she also enjoyed her status among her peers as a naval wife with a steady income (as opposed to wives of civilians dependent on day-wages in a time of widespread unemployment) and with no man on hand who would have to be deferred to for domestic decisions.

I do not recall, for instance, my father being around in the autumn of 1939 when I went through the trauma of being in hospital. It was a shattering experience, and for years was my definition of terror. In later life I discovered that many of my contemporaries went through the same miserable experience of having a mastoidectomy, since it was a sort of fashionable thing for boys of our age to have if we showed the slightest sign of earache. It was not serious, of course, and I was only in hospital for a matter of days, but for us kids it was an unforgettable horror.

I was taken to the Gosport War Memorial, a very Twentieth Century cottage hospital that boasted two main storeys of brick with cream-coloured stucco rendering, leafy grounds with monkey puzzle trees and a lawned frontage under an enormous clock dedicated to the memory of a local parson, Canon Guy Landon, ticking time away over the front door. I've always thought that was making a rather unnecessary point about mortality.

The wide corridors with their polished woodblock floors reeked of surgical spirit, a scent that even now can sometimes hit me with a paralysing sense of foreboding. The place was presided over by nurses with shiny, clean faces and wirebrush hair, mostly ginger, who wore stiff aprons and wide, ungainly skirts so that they didn't look like women at all, but a kind of in-between creature neither mother nor girl, nor man.

In those days parents were not encouraged to spend time with their children on the wards. Mum brought me into the hospital, a nurse took me by the hand, Mum left (no doubt in tears), and I was taken into a ward, undressed and put to bed. My teddy bear was sniffed over and thrown in a locker.

"He won't like it in there," I wail.

Silence. Nurse walks away. The boy in the next bed says: "Don't cry. They get cross and shout at you if you cry."

The rest is a series of disjointed nightmares: a man in white holding something over my face that looked like a big tea strainer, a sweet sickly smell; waking up wrapped in bandages. Nurses being cross with me because I had crapped in the bed. Nurses complaining about this to my mother; she trying to apologise.

A nurse who brought me little sandwiches with apple and sugar in them. Being given a book to draw in and a set of beautiful coloured pencils which I hardly used for colouring because I admired them so much, their slender lines, shiny surfaces, neat points, the colours — red, yellow, blue, green. Their perfect balance in my hand....I spent more time admiring them than I did using them. But the best feeling of all was going home and having a big fuss made of me.

Uncle Alf brought my old brown and green pram into the back sitting room at our house in Avenue Road and set it up with my rocking horse — a grey as I recall — so that, with hood up, it looked like a prairie schooner from the wild west. I used to sit in the pram with Ted, my bear, riding shotgun beside me and with a 'Yi-ha' and 'Giddyup' and a lash with the whip, Rocky would plunge off scattering redskins left and right.

My 'podner' Ted and I re-lived incidents from the Western comics that came my way. My hero was Buck Jones of the cowboy films and I dreamed of wearing a cowboy outfit with a bandana round my neck, just like his. Fashions change. The typical western dress of my heroes would be laughed at now. Around the late Fifties, cowhands stopped tucking their trousers into their knee-high boots and left off wearing weskits. Anyway those woolly trousers long ago gave way to jeans. Somehow they've hung on to the stetson and the bandana that I loved so much.

The centre of entertainment for families was the wireless. My father had bought a stylish black and silver Echo model. It had a circular façade, with a lighted tuning dial offering romantic foreign stations such as Paris, Vienna and even Moscow, and we quite often listened to the English language commercial stations such as Radio Luxembourg and Fécamp, in Normandy, home of the Benedictine distillery. Along with my infant pals I was signed up as an Ovaltine-y and happily joined in the show's opening song:

"We are the Ovaltine-ies
Happy girls and boys...."

A BBC show we never missed was Sunday evening's *Hi Gang!* presented by the American showbiz couple Ben Lyon and Bebe Daniels, dearly loved because they came over to Britain and threw in their lot with us at a time when there was quite a lot of nervous, middle-class traffic going the other way. The nation never forgot them and they were still working with the BBC into the 1960s.

Ben would open the show by saying 'Hi, Gang' and we'd shout 'Hi, Ben,' back at the radio. Then there would follow a lot of gags based on the premise that the suave and debonair Vic Oliver was for ever trying to cut Ben out and move in on Bebe. For its time some of the cross-talk and the comedy routines were quick-fire stuff.

Vic Oliver was the old smoothie every woman recognised as a philanderer, but of course he had continental charm, impeccable manners, and a Viennese accent to thrill any romantic English gal. Despite having a very limited set of gags and a tendency to stick to the same old material, he was never short of work on the monopolistic BBC — maybe the fact that he was Winston Churchill's son-in-law, married to Sarah, had something to do with it.

Vic would stroll up to the microphone with violin under his arm and build the tension by offering to play it....(cue Viennese accent) "I vish I hatt a Palm Court." Then, to the orchestra: "You start and I'll try to ketch you up...."

He'd play a note or two then interrupt: "Rubadubdub three men in a tub...How insanitary!" Or "Thirty days haff September, April, June and November; all the rest haff thirty-one....I ask you, is zat fair?"

According to his publicity his father had been very rich, a Hungarian count or something, who lost everything in the Great War. Apparently he had a wardrobe with a different suit for every day of the year. I always wanted to ask Vic Oliver — was this 365 suits, or 366 to cover the leap years?'

**********

Like a lot of kids in my class at Newtown infants school, a stone's throw from our house, I was to all intents fatherless. However I did have the undivided attention of my mother, and this was probably our closest time together. Conscious that I lacked what later became known as 'a male role model' she tried to give me the physical jobs around the house, like lighting the fire under the copper for the weekly wash, or chopping firewood. We spent a lot of time playing games together, or reading comics or children's books, but she also did her best to teach me how to box.

Like most of the boys in the street I had a pair of Boys' Boxing Gloves and one day Mum showed up with a matching pair — for her. Since her hands were not much bigger than mine they were a reasonable fit, too.

"I'm going to teach you to box, just like real fighters. I used to watch Alf and Bill sparring when I was a girl, so I know a bit about it," she told me.

"Tell you what, we'll have proper boxers' names. You be Darkie Pete and I'll be, um....Ginger Bill."

I had my doubts about this.

"But Mum I can't go punching you...."

She held up an open glove.

"Go on. Hit that." I gave her hand a sharp tap, and she promptly swung the other glove and slapped me under the ear.

"Come on," she said. "You can pull your punches....and don't hit me in the face, OK?"

We finished up more shadow boxing than anything else. I did learn a bit about ducking and weaving....but essentially it was something we did for fun. I do remember we laughed a lot.

**********

The grocer's shop she sent me to most often on errands was in Avenue Road, down on the opposite corner from where we lived. It had the name HUGHES over the front. My mother may have called it 'Hues', but to me it was 'U-jees'. After all I was still learning to read.

U-jees was a big, raw chap with an orange face and veins showing, bluish red. Maybe the face of a man who ate too much meat.

"Please, Mum sent me for a quarter of tea."

"Who said that?" the man asks, peering over the counter, playing to the gallery, his audience a couple of giggling women, in aprons and with their hair loose, signifying that it was early in the day.

"Oh, it's an ugly, little dwarf. Have you got any money, short pants?" Old U-jees had a wonderful sense of humour.

I place my small handful of coppers on the counter, near to tears and knowing the ordeal is only beginning.

"Didn't I see you kissing Margaret Morris last night?" More titters from his audience of two.

And so it went on. He felt free to give us kids a few lashes from his tongue every time one of us went in there. I hated that man so much, even now it is hard to write dispassionately. It was the start of a beautiful hateship, not just with U-jees, but all corner shopkeepers.

The shop on the corner of Queen's Road and Sydney Road, opposite Hayward's Bakery, was Mrs Moss's — but later on there was sometimes a man there I didn't know. He was tall, wore a brown overall and glasses. The shop was full of a vanilla scent composed, I imagined then, of soap and ice cream. I used to come across it sometimes in small corner shops, or something very like it, and I can taste it in my nose now as I think of it. It conjures up the things they sold, farthing sherbet dips, little lead soldiers, Mazawatee tea, hard nibbly cheese, rich plum jam, and Oxo cubes we used to lick and suck instead of the sweets we couldn't buy because they were rationed.

"Turn out your pockets!"

"What for?"

"You know, you little devil. Turn 'em out."

My Saturday threepence, a piece of string, two small conkers, a treasured piece of putty. No stolen goods. No apology from him either. Just a "Hurrumph!" that said "maybe not this time, but I don't trust you," as he pushes me none too gently towards the door.

Mrs Munday, who kept the sweetshop further up Queen's Road, on the corner opposite the Shakespeare Hall, was a round, motherly lady with small, rimless granny glasses. My Uncle Bill, my mother's brother, was sweet on her daughter Muriel. They 'walked out' together, as the saying was.

"Look, son, these are new," she said, revealing the first Mars bar I'd ever seen. This was just after the war began and I expect it cost a halfpenny. Another novelty she shoved my way was Barrage Balloon toffee. The makers had the bright idea of putting topical wartime names on their sweets. Everyone loved those blossoming gas-filled, silver-grey elephants floating over the town — we had two locally, one in Walpole Park and another in St Vincent Field on the other side of the railway line. Unfortunately the toffee was gritty and tasted truly awful.

"Have you tried my jelly babies? Go on take one," Mrs Munday would offer, or it might be custard tips, or a striped humbug.

Treats like this softened me up, until I was fool enough to confide in her that I had a girl friend, as opposed to a girlfriend, you understand. Lilias and I had had a fight, over the use of a tricycle, and I also confided that to smiling Mrs Munday.

The snake. She waited until I came in when the shop was full before telling them all: "He's had a bust up with Lilias Reid. Apparently she mentioned marriage." Their horrible laughter followed me down Queen's Road and stung for a good many years, too.

# Chapter Four
## Ferry Gardens Dogfight and the Mark of Adolf

On my fifth birthday, in June 1940, I was given a pair of toy binoculars which immediately became my most treasured possession. I used to stand on the garden wall, steadying myself against the clothes post (which carried the washing line) and sweep the skies looking for aeroplanes, hoping to see a Spitfire and a Messerschmidt shooting it out over our heads in what we called a dogfight.

By some miracle the binoculars were still unbroken on a day in the August holidays that Grandpa took me for our usual walk down to the gardens by the ferry, across the harbour from Portsmouth, a favourite place for him to pick up his bets on racing days. He met a lot of people he knew and stopped to chat.

"Lovely day, Mr Ferré," most of them said. It was, too, with clear blue skies and a few puffs of cloud moving slowly in a light breeze. Good flying weather perhaps. Ever since June, when France had 'packed it in' as Gosport people termed it, everybody in England seemed to be expecting the German army to land in force along the south coast. Even when it wasn't mentioned out loud it was on everyone's mind.

We must have got to the gardens at about 10 o'clock and, lovely day or not, suddenly we were in the middle of our first air-raid. I remember Grandpa telling people afterwards that the Bofors anti-aircraft gun near the ferry started firing some time before the siren sounded.

The first unbelievably loud bang from that gun hammered our ears like a blacksmith bashing an anvil. Everyone stood paralysed by shock.

Then suddenly people were running for the air-raid shelter, and a crowd of them were helping Grandpa and me along, shouting at each other to hurry up and get under cover. This wasn't a practice. This was real. The war had come to Gosport.

The Bofors gun in its sandbagged pit in the ferry gardens banged away at the sky, as did every gun on every ship in the harbour. The noise itself was petrifying. I saw black puffs of smoke appear high in the air and, despite being scared by the noise, I wanted to take a closer look through my binoculars.

"There's no time for that. Got to get into the shelter," Grandpa shouted. A young man lifted me up and started running with me held tightly to him. Over his shoulder I could see the barrage balloons hoisted over the ships and, just as we reached the shelter, a black plane sweeping above the buildings on the Portsmouth side.

Someone yelled out: "Look, look....it's Jerry" and we all stopped to watch. The aircraft raced along with tiny puffs of smoke appearing all round it. There was a sudden burst of flame in the sky and the remains of a blazing barrage balloon drifted down, as the black plane headed out over the sea towards the Isle of Wight.

The crowd came to its senses and piled into the shelter. They were all talking at once, yelling at each other over the ear-splitting, heart-stopping hammer blows of the guns. Scared, but also excited. A couple of young men stationed themselves by the door of the shelter and every now and again stepped out for a quick look — ignoring the women in the shelter who kept shouting: "Don't be a fool. Get back inside!"

The men kept up a commentary that was repeated from mouth to mouth down the shelter.

"There's another plane" — "Another plane." "Think they've dropped a bomb" — "Dropped a bomb."

One of the men shouted: "There's a plane been hit. Smoke's pouring from the engine. I can see a parachute coming down. Must be the pilot. Be lucky to get down through all this gunfire."

"Probably drop in the water and drown," a woman suggested.

"Is it the invasion, do you think?" people were asking each other.

"I can't hear the church bells," said one of the older men. "They'd ring the bells if it was the invasion."

A woman said: "Be typical of Jerry to sneak up without warning." And everyone laughed, as if the Germans were obliged to make sure someone rang the churchbells before they started marching up the beach.

I have no idea how long it lasted; I don't suppose any of us could have been certain.

When the all-clear siren wailed out its long, drawn-out note we went, thankfully, outside. People seemed reluctant to go home and hung around talking about the raid. This was something new all right. Gosport would have to start coming to terms with this. So this was war. On the doorstep, or more accurately, bang overhead.

Even Grandpa, usually a shy man, had plenty to say; until he realised the rest of the family would be worried about us.

A kindly taxi driver offered us a free ride home. As we drove up Queen's Road the driver suddenly said: "Hello, something's up." People were standing about in groups at their front gates.

Grandpa thanked the driver and hurried me up the path. He raised the knocker on his front door at 123 Queen's Road — and the door collapsed inwards. Inside, the house was a wreck, rubble and broken glass everywhere. We finally noticed there was no glass in any of the windows. Shreds of lace curtains hung about the shattered Venetian blinds that Grannie was so proud of.

The neighbours gathered round.

"Where are they?" Grandpa shouted.

"They're all right, don't worry," they said, and led us to the pub on the corner, the Queen's Hotel. My mother ran out to meet us and scooped me up in her arms.

"Thank God he's safe," said Grannie, kissing the top of my head. She sat down, nursing a glass of stout and I saw her face and clothes were covered in dust.

"We were buried alive, Alf," she told my grandfather, a sob in her voice. "The ARP and the neighbours have only just dug us out." Grandpa hugged her to him.

My uncle Alf handed his father a welcome glass of whisky.

"House a few doors down took a direct hit," he said. "Dunno if anyone was in there. In the blast a ton of rubble fell on our shelter. We were all in there."

"Then where's Bill?" Grandpa asked, looking round for his younger son.

"I'm here, Dad," he called, hurrying over. "I had to go and have my head stitched at the ARP post. They got their hands full with all the casualties...."

Alfie Waterloo, the landlord of the Queen's, handed him a pint of ale. We watched him take a deep pull.

"Look," Uncle Bill said pointing to his forehead, "look at this cut. I'm going to have a scar shaped just like a swastika!"

Alfie's wife Maude went over to examine his cut; after all it was the street's first war wound. "Well, Bill," she announced in the way that landladies have, "you've got the mark of Adolf, all right. Let's hope it's a good luck charm."

Everyone laughed. War had come to Gosport suddenly. Many people had been injured, some had been killed. My grandparents and uncles were homeless. And yet they could laugh?

Grannie, perhaps remembering World War I, was the first to take it in.

"Seems like there's not going to be any civilians in this war," she said. She sipped her glass of stout, crossed herself and added: "God help us all."

My mother and I went with the rest of the family to survey the damage to their home. We went down the alley at the back that Queen's Road shared with Blake Road. I saw a deep hole in the ground a few houses down from Grannie's. Where there had been tidy gardens with neat flower-beds, there was now brick rubble and brown earth. The little dividing garden walls were gone, bricks strewn everywhere. Grannie's air-raid shelter was still mostly buried. Most of the house windows were smashed, and shards of glass lay all over the place.

We picked our way up to the back door, hanging off its hinges. The kitchen was a mess of broken crockery, ripped wallpaper and smashed furniture. The force of the blast had turned the table upside down. The ceiling had buried the gas cooker.

A warden in Civil Defence uniform came over.

"This your place, Mother?" he said gently to Grannie. She nodded through her tears and my Mum moved up to comfort her.

"We've had to turn the gas off," the warden said. "But you've got water on. I expect we'll be sealing these damaged houses off soon, but you're welcome to get some of your stuff. Be very careful, though, specially if you go upstairs."

In the event Grannie and Grandpa came home with us, while the uncles began organising salvage operations. By the next day the houses were cordoned off and Grannie was looking around for a new place to rent. Meanwhile they were going to move in with their other daughter, my Auntie Gert.

We later heard that one of the neighbours, Mrs Amy Utting who was in her fifties, had been killed by the blast; dozens of others had been injured. Wartime censorship meant rumours were rife — a group of young sailors had been machine-gunned as they ran across the sports field at the navy training school HMS St Vincent, no more than a couple of hundred yards away on the other side of the railway line; the airfield at Lee had been bombed and more sailors and civilians killed....

In fact — as the facts later emerged, years later in some cases — a dive bomber had attacked our friendly barrage balloon site in the sports field and a direct hit killed ten airmen in their dugout — official reports listed them as Cpl A R Barrell (33), Cpl A Croker, Cpl R W Hollister (29), LAC C H Chilcott (20), LAC G. McElrea (19), LAC H Reed (19), AC1 A E Grant (42), AC1 A J Smith (26), AC2 H W Hale (21), AC2 R F Hill (21).

Two Gosport groundsmen were also killed: Herbert William Gatesby (64) of Oval Gardens, and Charles Hastings (44) of Felix Road.

Two RAF men survived the attack: LACs Bill Kemp and Frank Offord. Apparently they had gone out of the shelter to watch the action — and when the dive bomber struck, hurled themselves into a 4ft slit trench. They were buried alive — but survived. A memorial tablet telling the story of the raid now stands respectfully at the entrance to the sports field.

Official records of civilian deaths also list Mrs Charlotte Mogg of Crossways, Forton.

And the Luftwaffe returned for another attack a few days later when nine men at Lee-on-the-Solent, a workman from Ireland at the Wimpey works in Rowner, and another man in Middlecroft Lane, off Ann's Hill Road, were all killed.

By then seven houses — Grannie's and three others on each side of it — were condemned as irreparable, to be pulled down to make a cleared bomb site. It was the first of about a dozen that would appear in the streets near Queen's Road.

# Chapter Five
# The Night they Blitzed the Ritz

My mother also had a spell in hospital at this time, during which I was placed in the care of my Grannie, with great assistance from my oldest female cousin Freda.

She used to take me out in my pushchair, presumably to give Grannie a chance to 'get on' as they used to say about housework in those days. This included cooking for herself and husband Alfred, my uncles Alf and Bill, and me. From that time onwards Freda was known in the family as Baby John's second mother. She was quite a character then, and she still is. I don't see her often enough but whenever I do I still call her My Second Mother, which seems to please her, though it is not a job any woman would wish on another unless extremely spiteful.

Obviously she was an important early influence, complementing Grannie. One clear memory stands out: Freda pushing me in the pushchair in the grounds of the War Memorial Hospital and lifting me up to see Mum over a wooden fence. Mum wore a dressing gown over her nightie and was sitting rather forlornly in a deck chair, unsteadily taking the air after radium treatment for a growth in her neck.

As far as I know that was the only time my mother was in hospital until her final illness at the age of 80.

I cannot imagine why my family, normally stroppy where their rights were concerned, did not make a fuss about not being able to bring 'her boy in to see his poor mother. After all she might never have a chance to hold him and kiss and hug her baby ever again.'

So my convalescent mother, reckoned not to be up to a regular job, but resenting not having a bit of extra cash, jumped to respond to a plea from the Royal Navy for local folk, preferably with naval connections, to take in young sailors as lodgers. This offered a useful ten shillings a week in return for accommodation, meals when the men were off duty and some dhobi-ing (washing clothes).

I was duly warned that two sailor boys were coming to live with us. They were to have a bedroom each and my cot would be put in Mum's room. I was warned never to set foot in either room except in the extremely unlikely event of being invited. On pain of....well pain, probably administered with the back of the hairbrush she was waving in a threatening manner to help fix the room embargo in my tiny mind.

To Mum, I suppose, the sailor boys were a godsend, product of some distant star and not like other human males. Few of the new naval-wife landladies, dazzled by the cash offer, gave much deep thought to what they were taking on. In their minds they saw young, smartly uniformed seamen, in tiddly suits ready for Admiral's parade.

What they got were spotty youths with families that loved them, untidy at home, none too house-trained yet, with hearts of gold and little brothers to whom they were heroes, if not gods.

Our two, Jock and Jim, came in at the front gate in uniform, including their distinctive winter-rig dark blue round hats, and slung over their shoulders, the space-saving navy kitbags that doubled as hammocks. They were amazed to learn they were to have the exclusive use of a whole room (8ft by 11ft) to themselves, a luxury undreamt of by most working-class lads, let alone to recruits in a service that traditionally jammed hundreds of sailors into the lower decks of men o' war....with only 14 inches of space each.

And indeed this tradition was maintained in barracks ashore. A kindness, I presume, on the part of a grateful Admiralty who did not wish their men to suffer the shock of space-deprivation when their turn came to go to sea.

For me their doors were never shut. I suppose I was a link with the world they'd known before the navy. Jim was a little dour — the first Scot I'd ever met. At first he was hard to understand but five-year-olds are very quick to learn and I soon became my mother's interpreter:

Jock: Forby ahno be un ick wikken, yken, Missus.

Me: I won't be in this weekend, Missus, I'm on duty at the barracks.

Mum: Okay, thanks for letting me know. Is there anything you might need in the way of washing or ironing?

Jock: Aw uts awfa bonny o' ye — bot forby ul muss yer kookun.

Mum beamed. I had no need to interpret the last bit.

A look of understanding passed between Jock and me — he was just being nice. No-one who had tried it would ever quote cooking as one of my mother's many accomplishments. Still, there was a war on and when you are hungry....you butter up the cook.

The boys became for me the living embodiment of Darkie Pete and Ginger Bill. They showed me how to box, first making sure I laced up my Boys' Boxing Gloves properly. It probably saved them from harm as I hurled myself at the victim, arms going like windmills and raining blows on any part of the body I could hit.

Over the months, I figure Jock and Jim learned more about self-defence from me, once they realised that I was the real enemy at this stage of the war.

Also on the agenda was Snakes and Ladders, that wonderful game for kids. And best of all, table tennis. We bought a set from Woolworth's that contained a net with two supports that screwed to each side of the kitchen table, a couple of bats with sandpaper surfaces, and half a dozen celluloid balls.

The poor sailor boys were expected to play at least once a day. It must have been seriously tedious for them: if I hit a return at all, it would go wildly in any direction – and then my opponent was expected to crawl about the floor helping to retrieve the ball, usually from under the gas stove, or jammed between the wall and the built-in copper used to boil up the wash every Monday.

What we ate in those days I have largely blotted out of memory. Boiled eggs and toast and jam figured prominently, plus a sort of cheese in a box, called I think Velveeta, that you had to spread on your bread. Dinners, whether taken at lunchtime or in the evening, meant a stew, a meat pie, or 'a nice bit of fish.'

Mum and the boys had plenty to occupy them without dwelling unduly on the war. Earlier fears of invasion faded as the RAF — miraculously as it seemed at the time — gained the upper hand in the Battle of Britain and cleared the daylight skies of German raiders.

But in the autumn came the terror of the night attacks and the Blitz. The fury of the bombing on London was added to the unending nightmare of the war at sea, especially the battle of the Atlantic, our lifeline for food and war material under American Lease-Lend. It seems to me the only real weapon Britain had was the stubborn refusal of its tribes to see sense and give in.

This is how we lived. And how we survived. Stories of the night bombing attacks on British cities dominated chat over the fence or in the shops. Us kids just got on with collecting our shrapnel. Most of us could tell at a glance whether a jagged chunk of steel in the gutter came from an anti-aircraft shell, or perhaps, more fancifully, a fragment of a German high explosive bomb.

I once overhead two older boys discussing this:

Big Boy: No it wasn't a firebomb. It blew up dinnit? It was an HE, high explosive bomb.

Little brother: So what's a low explosive bomb like then?

Of course, Jock and Jim could be relied upon to add to my collection anything they found. My father, like most of the other Dads, was a hero too far away to get his due but I had two live warriors living in. They were only 18, though to me they were heroes. Jock, short and dark, from Dunfermline, suffered a lot with his ears. There was a lot of it about in those days. My mother would warm a pair of his thick seaman's socks by the fire.

"When you go to bed, fold them into a pad and put it under your ear. The heat will ease the pain and you'll be able to get off to sleep," she told him.

Jim was tall and fair and so homesick he spent all his time writing letters. I felt sorry for both of them, though it didn't stop me badgering them to play with me.

At this time at the age of five, apart from the lovely Lilias, I had a number of friends about my own age including Buster, the boy next door, and Sylvia the pretty girl who lived next to the railway goods yard at the top of Avenue Road. Not unnaturally, therefore, I was unhappy at having a little, runny-nosed kid of only three-and-a-half foisted on me. It was the sort of deal that young mothers cooked up between them. My mother would say to one of them: "Would you mind having John tomorrow morning for a couple of hours? I've got a bit of shopping to do."

Of course, she would then owe the favour of a return morning's child-minding. And that is how I came to be penned up with Tommy in my own garden, with no way of escape.

He was big for his age, robust on his stumpy little legs and his large head was covered in blond curls. All the mothers, grown-up girls and old ladies said he looked like an angel.

I found out the first day he came to 'play' with me that he was more of a devil.

"Here's Tommy come to play with you," Mum said, leading him out into the garden, followed by his mother, a thin creature who didn't look much older than some of the big girls at our school. I'd heard Mum telling the lady next door she'd heard the girl was married to a Royal Marine who had been posted to Plymouth — regarded by Portsmouth families as a disaster — leaving her to cope on her own with no family living near.

The other mums all felt sorry for her, especially since she also had three other children, one older and two younger than Tommy. The neighbours often took her parcels of left-off clothes. Which might have explained why Tommy was dressed in shiny black shoes and a sort of silky frock tucked into drooping rompers.

"I hope he's not going to be any bother," offered his mother with something in her voice that suggested different.

"Oh, bless him," mine cooed. "He's so sweet. He'll be all right here in the garden.

"Now you play with him nicely and don't let him get all dirty, John," she added, giving me one of her stern looks.

Our garden was separated from the back of the house by a rickety trellis with a creeper growing up it. It served to screen off the outside lavatory built into the back of the house. All the houses were constructed like that, and every now and then a visitor would wonder out loud why the lav wasn't fitted up the other way round with the door inside the house, so you didn't have to go outside in the rain to use the place. It was just one of life's mysteries. Still is.

A narrow path ran down to the alley we shared with the backs of other bay-and-forecourt houses in Queen's Road. On the right of our garden path was a narrow strip with a few flowers in it, some climbing up the trellis mounted on top of the wall. The bigger plot on the left was a stretch of bare earth down as far as the newly-installed Anderson air-raid shelter, half buried in the garden earth.

This was our playground. I had a tricycle to ride up and down the path, or outside along the back alleys, some wheeled toys — a tin lorry or fire engine — to push around the paved area outside the back door, and a bucket and spade to dig in the earth, the favourite thing in dry weather. Buster and I had tunnelled all over that patch. We'd have spent all day out there if they'd let us.

Keeping Tommy clean meant digging was out of the question. So I had to share the tin lorry and the fire engine with him. I offer him the lorry.

"Me want injin," he says.

"You dunno what to do yet, " I tell him. " We've got to put a fire out. You watch what I do and then you can have a go in a minute." I was doing my best here. I begin fitting the little firemen into their places and ringing the bell.

"Me want injin," he insists in his whiney, singsong voice with the lisp that the women loved and I want to choke off at the throat.

"Play with the lorry for now. Have the engine in a minute."

The angel pinches up his face, grabs the lorry and hurls it straight at my chest. The blow brings a tear to my eye and I reach out to slap him. He dodges away and gives me a stinging kick on the leg.

"Want injin!" he screams. What happened to loveable?

I grab his arm with some idea of cooling him down. And at that point Mum, hearing his screams, rushes out of the house.

"What are you doing to him?" she shouts at me. Giving me a good shaking.

As I open my mouth I have a sudden, early dawning that I am on a hiding to nothing. A glance at Tommy shows he is the complete angel again, sobbing and bravely biting back the tears.

"Want injin," he lisps, reaching out for it.

"Let him share your toys, John," says my mother. "And don't bully him again. Play nicely, like I said. I've got to get on."

I picked up the lorry and pushed it about the concrete, doing my best to ignore the little snot. He shoved the fire engine hard across the yard so that it ran into the wall. Then he started pulling the little men out and hurling them down the garden. I sighed and patiently went to pick them up.

This little game was repeated over and over for some time, mostly in silence.

It wasn't enough for Tommy. He waited until I put my hand out to replace the toy driver in the fire engine, lunged at me and sank his teeth into my flesh.

My yelp of agony brought my mother out of the back door like a jack-in-the-box ready to batter me. Tearfully I held up my hand to show her the marks of his sharp baby teeth.

She stood looking from me to the angel and back again. Then she took us both inside the house. Under her eyes we spent the rest of the morning with picture books. I noticed she hardly went near Tommy. I think she was as nervous of him as I was.

Certainly she was relieved when school restarted and I went back for the mornings. The couple of afternoons we had Tommy to visit, she was as careful as I was not to cross the monster.

He must have missed us, though. Because one lunchtime when my mother collected me from school we found the back door wide-open and half-eaten sweets and biscuits strewn all over the kitchen. My precious toy sword was lying in the yard, snapped in two, the head of my clockwork soldier on horseback had been wrenched off, and — here was a clue — the bite marks in a half-chewed and abandoned sugar mouse showed two clear rows of baby teeth.

Mrs Mills, Buster's mother next door, later confirmed that she'd seen Tommy running down the path and into the alley. I wanted to run down to his house and punch the rotten snot. My sword, the best one in the street! Why my horse soldier? I'd never get another one; clockwork toys had disappeared in 1939.

My mother was angry too: "The sneaky little devil. I shall have to have words with her. Fancy letting a kid that age wander about like that. What does she think she's about?"

Buster's mum shook her head and made suitable tutting noises.

Mum never did 'have words' with Tommy's mum. Soon after, a couple of weeks before Christmas 1940, a German bomb wiped out all three kids, their mother and father. The word was that their shelter at 79 Avenue Road had taken a direct hit and they had had no chance. Another young mother and her baby, apparently sharing the shelter, were also killed.

The terrifying night raids of December 5 and 6 were among the earliest — and deadliest — so far on the Portsmouth area. In Gosport the bombing was concentrated on a small area on either side of the railway line. The casualties were horrendous: the War Memorial Hospital in Gosport, and the hospitals in Portsmouth, had their first real blooding for what was to come through the long months of air warfare on civilians.

Christmas that year was overshadowed as dozens of families mourned their dead, comforted injured relatives, tried to find somewhere to live, or made makeshift repairs to their homes.

Apart from the families in Avenue Road, the death list in Gosport included the Hunt family of 135 Forton Road, parents Alfred and Kathleen and their three sons David (18), Alfred (15), and Roy (11); Maud Pitt (65) and her daughter Ivy (49) next door at 133; a couple from Belgium, George and Minnie Van Quackebreke at 137; and Fredrick Gilbert (60) of 205 Forton Road; as well as William Candy (34) of 52 Albert Street and Violet Topp (49) a widow in Railway Cottages, just the other side of the tracks from Avenue Road.

Tommy was the first child to die in our street. I suppose most of the mothers suffered the same, silent, choked-up feeling that mine did. They didn't say much. It hit everyone too hard for that.

I finally, tearfully, told Mum that I wished I had been nicer to Tommy.

"We all wish that, son," she said.

**Note:** the grave of Tommy and his family at Ann's Hill cemetery in Gosport is marked by a simple military memorial to his father Corporal Thomas Stevens of the Princess Louise Kensington Regiment. At the time civilian and military dead were listed separately — even if they died in the same incident.

\*\*\*\*\*\*\*\*\*\*

As winter wore on the fading afternoon light saw Mum and her neighbours glance anxiously at the sky more and more often. A sort of waiting quiet fell over Avenue Road and even the shunting of the railway trucks became muted.

Sunset in the western sky flared more brilliantly as the darkness of the east came relentlessly on. The mothers, grandmothers and the old men re-learned the fear of night.

I would run the few dozen yards home from Newtown Infant School in Grove Avenue to Mum waiting with the front door open. She'd look up at the last streaks of colour above, cross herself and softly say the evening prayer:

"Lighten our darkness we beseech thee, O Lord,
And in thy great mercy guard us from all perils and dangers of this night,
For the sake of thy only son, our Saviour, Jesus Christ. Amen."

One of that kind of day — possibly Friday January 10 1941 — Jock and Jim had both eaten their dinner in the mess as they were on duty at the barracks. At six, with Jock still working, Jim sat down with Mum and me for a navy-style tea with hot buttered toast and a slice of cake, made using honey instead of rationed sugar, and chopped dates rather than currants and sultanas.

I listened to Children's Hour on the BBC, and after tea poor Jim played table tennis with me before we all sat down for the rest of the evening, with Mum knitting, Jim reading and me with my comics, round a bright coal fire.

Most people stayed in. The radio was not up to much. Unless it was Jack Warner and Garrison Theatre — 'Hey, mind my bike' was his catchphrase. You heard someone repeat it almost every day.

Some brave souls, noting that it was a nice dry night, ventured out to the pictures, the Forum in Stoke Road, the Ritz in Walpole Road, backing onto the moat in Walpole Park, and the Cri (Criterion) in Forton Road. The Forum and the Ritz were newly-built, real picture palaces. The Cri was older and known as the bug hutch....

Suddenly Mum was gently shaking me: "Wake up son. Get up. We've got to go to the shelter." It was pitch dark but for the dim light of her torch dancing around the walls and ceiling as she moved about, picking up things she wanted to take with her. I could hear the wail of the siren we called Moaning Minnie. Its mournful rise and fall always brought a bolt of anxiety in even the bravest — still the most scary sound I've ever heard.

"Is it a raid, Mum?" I asked. "Yes. Come on. Get up. Down to the shelter. Here, put your dressing gown on. Hurry up, do." It wasn't like her to be panicky. Then as I stumbled from bed, came the loudest bang I'd ever heard. I thought my ears had burst. It tore through the air of the bedroom and a vase fell off the mantlepiece and smashed in the grate.

Mum scooped me up and rushed down the stairs sliding her back down the wall to help support me. At the bottom Jim met her, seized me up, ran to the kitchen and threw open the back door. He staggered back as if he'd been hit, as a second paralysing bang shook the house.

Jock appeared from the garden: "It's all right. It's our anti-aircraft gun firing," he said. He meant to reassure us I know, but the noise was too close, and too much to bear.

"Mum, where's Mum?" I whimpered and wriggled round in Jim's arms trying to see where she was. He braced himself and darted out into the garden, following Jock down the path to our dugout. The night was full of noise and great beams from searchlights reached high into the sky. Between the crash of gunfire I heard the drone of engines. German bombers.

Mum was suddenly there shining her torch.

"Get in, get in," she ordered the boys, as she fumbled with the latch on the shelter. Jim tumbled down the little steps and dumped me none too gently on one of the bunks that lined each side. Mum followed and established herself on the bunk at the back of the shelter; Jock smacked the door smartly to, and switched on the emergency light. In the gloom. Mum looked around her: "Jesus, I hope this place is safe." The noise of battle seemed louder down here.

"Are they bombs?" I whispered and Mum moved over to comfort me, holding me close and smoothing my hair.

Jock whispered: "No son, that's oor guns firing at Jerry planes. We've got a Bofors gun trundlin' roun' the streets — it keeps yon pilots frae coming too low to drop their bombs."

Apart from explosives, the bombs were made with fins and vents that set up a shrieking noise as they fell. It was a terror weapon, to instil panic. It worked well for the Luftwaffe in Poland and France.

They used to say you never heard the bomb that had your name on it. So if you heard the whistle of the bomb coming down, you were safe. This time.

Suddenly there came a piercing whistle that sounded right outside. I stopped breathing....and so, I'm sure, did everyone else. Another huge bang tore the air apart. The shelter rocked and the ground seemed to shift. I thought I heard somebody shouting, then came the crash of falling masonry, maybe bricks, maybe someone's house. The air filled with dust. Mum and the boys fell silent staring at each other. She held me tighter.

In between the hideous noise of the guns and bombs, I heard a sound I knew.

"Listen," I whispered to Mum.

"What is it? What's the matter, son?"

"Hear that?"

"What?"

"It's someone playing table tennis...."

Mum looked at me anxiously. Was the boy's mind going?

Jim chuckled and leaned over me. "It's no a game they're playin', laddie. That's firebombs gangin' off. Makes a sort o' poppin' noise. Good job you're down here wit' us, eh?"

Later there came a lull in the night raid and I found I had fallen asleep in Jim's arms, he having relieved Mum, who in turn had dropped into an exhausted, semi-conscious state.

I looked sleepily round and realised that Jock was standing by the doorway looking up at the sky.

"Och, that's a awfy big fire over there," he said. "Some puir divils have copped ut bad, Ahm thinkin."

"Come back in, Jock," Mum told him, but at that moment the All Clear started to sound. She and the boys moved cautiously outside. Forgotten for the moment, I crawled along the bunk to look out.

The sky was the mother and father of all sunsets. A flaring crimson shot with tall spurts of fire, the air full of choking smoke and the bitter smell of burning. We were spitting and coughing, yet unable to look away from that brilliant sky.

"That fire's awful close," said Jim. "Maybe it's the barracks."

"Looks like a lot more of it over Pompey, too," Mum said.

"Hello...." a shout came from the alley behind us, "are you all right?" In the firelight we could see a helmeted air raid warden by the gate.

"Och we're fine," Jock said. Mum asked: "What's the big fire?"

"That's the Ritz, Missus. Too many incendiaries for the firemen to cope with. 'Fraid they had to let it burn itself out."

He added that there had been a big raid on Pompey. He wished us good luck and moved off down the alley. I was put back to bed, and the others faced up to another day.

**********

Poor old Pompey took a hammering. On January 10 1941 some 300 bombers attacked in waves. One of the first bombs was an unlucky hit on the electricity generating station, plunging all the ARP posts, police stations, hospitals and other vital services into darkness. Firestorms threatened to engulf the commercial area of King's Road and Palmerston Road in Southsea; top shops Handley's and Knight & Lee were soon well ablaze.

Fire service and ARP men deliberately dynamited buildings in some streets to create gaps, to slow the spread of flames. The heart of the city's shopping district, Commercial Road, was afire from end to end and notable shops like the Landport Drapery Bazaar, C&A, and Woolworth's were destroyed.

The Royal Hospital, and the Eye and Ear Hospital, were also bombed. Six churches and three cinemas were burnt out, and the 51-year-old Guildhall, the city's pride and joy, was a smouldering ruin. The Guildhall burned for 12 hours and it was several days before firemen could go into the devastated building.

After the raid the Lord Mayor announced that the city had withstood the onslaught of around 25,000 incendiary bombs.

Bits of horror stories about this disaster crossed the water to Gosport and I remember the family — especially Grannie and my mother — seemed to go into a sort of dry-eyed, numb shock as people we knew mourned the loss of parents, uncles, aunts, cousins, and some young children and babies. Then there were those who were still alive, but maimed or blinded. This was the reality of a bombing attack from the air.

Morale was a serious enough question to bring King George and Queen Elizabeth down to Pompey. I recall sitting with Mum in Grannie's house while she read to me the report of the visit in our weekly paper, the Hampshire Telegraph. She showed me a picture of the Queen chatting to ordinary mothers with turbans round their heads, holding babies; being invited in to a terrace cottage to see some war damage; or little kids lining up to meet the great lady — a day they'd always remember.

It was a traditional working-class metaphor come startlingly to life. From my earliest days my Grannie or my Mum would interrupt some mundane household chore — like laying up the table for tea — like this:

"Look at that sugar bowl — you forgot the sugar spoon. Go and get it out of the drawer. How's people supposed to put the sugar in — scoop it up with their 'ands? S'pose the Queen dropped in for tea, eh?" To which the usual family reply was:

"Very likely, I must say....Oh! Wotcher Yer Majesty, sorry didn't see you come in. Fancy a cuppa?" Accompanied by an elaborate curtsey.

And here it was — happening to ordinary folk in their own living room.

The paper mentioned an incident I've never forgotten: as the king and queen passed through the rubble of destroyed homes in once-proud streets lined mostly with mums and kids, someone called out "Are we downhearted?" and back came a roaring "NO!" We kept that cutting in a scrapbook for many years.

The Prime Minister Winston Churchill also came to visit the wounded city — his picture was in the Hampshire Telegraph, too. There was 'Winnie' wearing his navy-style uniform, smoking a big cigar and giving his trademark V-for-Victory salute. He brought with him an American — Roosevelt's special envoy to London, Harry Hopkins — to show the wily, old politician that Brits really could take the punishment and keep smiling (fingers crossed).

**********

The tall, modern brick walls of the burned-out Ritz stood throughout the war alongside the moat around the old town of Gosport as a sort of symbol of defiance, a reminder of good things past that might, one day, come round again.

Though it was boarded and sealed, we kids used to wriggle in through a 2ft by 1ft cavity in the brick wall, presumably that once housed a ventilator shaft, only a couple of inches above the ground on the east side of the building, hidden from any nosy adults by the Conservative Club across the alley. It was a bit frightening squeezing through, but well worth it because inside was a forbidden playground. There was debris everywhere, twisted blackened girders and all kinds of rubbish to sift through, looking for interesting finds.

We used to climb up iron rungs set in the walls and hang there high up, like bats. Or we'd climb right up above the level where the roof had been. Here there were narrow catwalks from which you could peer down into the moat, a good forty feet below.

Our little secret came out around 1944. A kid called Tony fell over the edge and thumped onto the asphalt outside the building, splitting his head open. I was standing only a few yards away and was astonished to see so much blood. Somebody ran for help, Tony was carted off to be stitched up — and the ventilator shaft was finally sealed off for ever.

**\*\*\*\*\*\*\*\*\*\***

It was a recognised phenomenon that the popping sound of an incendiary hitting the ground sounded very like a table tennis stroke. Incendiaries, or thermite bombs, were metal tubes about two feet long with small fins on the tail. In December 1941 thousands were dropped on London in the worst night-raid of the war. It nearly destroyed the whole of the City. By some miracle the raid, by 400 bombers in three waves, was pulled back just before an unstoppable fire storm would have been inevitable. Incendiaries also made a characteristic 'dent' in the pavement when they landed. Until the borough council started pouring cheap tarmac over the old craftsman-built paving of Gosport, I used to enjoy pointing out these wartime souvenirs to my children. There is one souvenir like this that you can still see — at

Holy Trinity Church on Trinity Green. On the night of the Ritz fire, Canon Cyril Barclay, the Vicar of Holy Trinity, was on fire-duty at his church. An incendiary bomb came though one of the tall nave windows. Father Barclay ran to the spot with his long-handled shovel, specially designed for the job, scooped up the sputtering firebomb and hurled it back out through the shattered window where it burned out harmlessly among the tombstones. Visitors can still see the burn marks on the church's parquet floor.

Avenue Road on the morning after the 1941 raid. All the wrecked homes were pulled down and cleared to create the biggest bombed site in Gosport: new territory where the Bomb Alley Kids built underground dens and cooked stews over open fires

# Chapter Six
# Buried Alive

After the first raid the previous August, my Grannie's house along with several others in Queen's Road were pulled down to leave a cleared bomb site — the first of three, as bombs brought more carnage to the street. My grandparents and my uncles, Alf and Bill, went to live at 32 Elmhurst Road, the next street off Stoke Road. This was a neat bay-and-forecourt house, painted cream like most of the houses in the street, with a tiny front garden which consisted mostly of dark green privet hedge. It was a few doors away from the Lawrence family's photographic studio, a local landmark.

So when our house was damaged in the Ritz night raid and we had to find somewhere else, Grannie was pleased to point out that the house next door to her was now vacant. Mum hurried down to Puttock and Blake estate agents to rent the place. No 34 was the left-handed version of Grannie's, the layout of which, of course, we were pretty familiar with as we were constantly in and out. In fact we had spent much of the previous Christmas there.

My best present had been a cowboy outfit — stetson, black and white check shirt, waistcoat (with sheriff's badge), dark-brown trousers with red-indian-style orange darts down the seam, and a gunbelt with cartridges, holster and a gleaming silver six-gun that fired caps. I was so proud of the outfit I could hardly bear to take it off at bedtime. As if we hadn't had quite enough of gunfire, I stalked about banging off caps and filling the air with gunsmoke.

Presumably to calm me down, Grannie decided I should have my photo taken. I think it was on Boxing Day that I was taken to the Lawrence studio in the conservatory and carefully posed. The photo was taken by David Lawrence — then a teenage apprentice photographer and part-time fireman, filling in until he became old enough to do his bit in the Royal Navy.

David Lawrence's picture of me on Boxing Day 1941

Our move from Avenue Road must have gone smoothly. I imagine Mum hired Rocky Norman's horse and cart, as people did then, and she had the willing help of sailor boy Jim to load stuff on board. Jock by this time had finished his training and was drafted to a ship. He left with everyone wishing him all the best and an unspoken 'God help you, lad' in their hearts.

But I do recall Grandpa playing a part in the move. He borrowed a gaily decorated red-and-green-painted handcart that I recognised from its pre-war life as the banana barrow that used to stand at the entrance to Walpole Park where a man with a red-neckerchief and a voice of brass used to holler "Ripe bananas — five a penny."

Bananas were never imported during the war, though shipments of oranges came in at regular intervals. I don't think anyone in Gosport had a glimpse of a banana from 1940 to 1945. The organisers of 'Wings for Victory Week' at the Connaught drill hall in 1944 did raffle a banana; a miserable, shrivelled up green thing not much bigger than a man's finger. It attracted the kids to marvel at it — but none of us bought a ticket.

So there was Grandpa with treasures Mum held too valuable to trust to Rocky and his mare, trundling his barrow with me and my pals whooping and running alongside, down Avenue Road, through the street-with-no-name (it had no houses in it — save for the side entrance to the Shakespeare Hall, venue of charity bazaars, sales of work, dances and weddings) and into Queen's Road.

Then 100 yards or so down towards Grandpa's favourite pub, the Albert — Grannie and Mum no doubt had dared him to even pause — and a swerve into Sydney Road by Hayward's bakery, the air here always fragrant with the smell of fresh bread, and finally a turn left at another pub, the Eagle, into Elmhurst Road.

It ran north-south and came out onto Stoke Road opposite the glorious Art Deco façade of the newish Forum Cinema, all ceramic tiles in soft pale colours and several pairs of glass doors right across the frontage.

Halfway down Elmhurst Road on the right-hand side was the Co-op bakery depot, with its electric delivery vans and milk floats. The yard served as a sort of class divide. To the south were the posh houses, the grand, red-brick mansions of 'Elm-hurst' Road, where the aspirational 'h' was always pronounced. The biggest had very extensive grounds with tall trees, such as Christchurch Vicarage, home of the awesome Reverend Sedgwick, and Leventhorpe, the near-palace of Dr John Skelton, surgeon and hero to every woman in town. Across the bottom of the road on the left-hand side was Bourton House, an imposing edifice whose tree-lined lawns ran right through to Queen's Road. For the duration of the war it had been taken over as a club for servicemen run by Toc H, the brainchild of the near-sainted Reverend Tubby Clayton.

In our half of the road, pronounced aspiration-free as 'Elm-erst' were the neatly-painted, respectable terraces of roomy bay-and-forecourt houses, with tidy slate roofs, a small but useful garden at the back, an outside toilet, of course, and only one cold water tap in the kitchen or scullery.

There were three bedrooms and a small box room, two principal rooms on the ground floor, the living room at the back with rather grand French windows — ours were painted a classy sky-blue, opening onto a small patio and the garden. The staircase ran across the house with a large cupboard under the stairs, and a side door off the passage, leading to the garden. The parlour was at the front of the house, used only when receiving visitors.

Almost as soon as we got there, sailor boy Jim received his draft, leaving Mum with a severe drop in income. But having her mother next door to look after me, she was soon looking round for a job. I must have thwarted this ambition because I recall almost as soon as we settled into the house, I came down with measles. In fact over the next few months, I got most of my childish ailments out of the way, having followed up with mumps and chicken pox. This led to Mum spending a lot of time entertaining me.

Having the two houses side by side allowed me to compare the different styles Grannie and Mum adopted in their furnishing and the bits and pieces of making a home. To take one example: the dining room suite. They each attached a lot of importance to the dining table, chairs and sideboard. Gran's was dark oak, in a rather older style, with barley twist legs; Mum's was markedly Art Deco in light oak which had a sort of greenish tinge.

The parlour furniture consisted of a sofa and two easy chairs, another smaller sideboard, and a couple of upright chairs, augmented to cope with any overflow of visitors by a couple of dining chairs brought in. They each had a small bookcase containing a variety of novels, Joseph Conrad, Agatha Christie, for instance, and some reference books on housekeeping or general home care the Modern Woman's Home Guide. And, of course, a Bible. In Grannie's case, it was a Family Bible with a family tree covering two or three generations, inked in on the fly-leaf.

The bedroom set-up consisted of a double or single bed, a couple of straight-backed chairs, a wardrobe, chest of drawers, and, for the women, a dressing table. In the case of guest or lodger, the top of the dressing table or a tall stand would be used for a basin of water and a pitcher for washing. The rest of the household used the kitchen, with a 'bungalow' bath, a long, deep tin bath, usually hung up outside until required for the weekly bath night, when it would be set up in the kitchen in summer and in front of the living room fire in winter. There was, of course, an open fireplace in every room except the kitchen, which originally held a cooking range, fuelled by coal and, by the Forties, a gas cooker if you were lucky.

The dressing table was a queenly place for applying make-up. A low seat with a set of drawers under a decorative glass top, with a mirror, or a set of three with a large tilting mirror in the middle, flanked by two narrow side mirrors. My mother and grandmother had almost identical sets. At the back of the dressing table were two decorative glass candlesticks, a couple of hand mirrors, and a ring holder, a glass dish with a central column for the rings. Mum's set was in green, of course, and Grannie's was a dark rose. However, both sets were in the fashionable Art Deco style.

As a child these things fascinated me. Mum had some costume jewellery which, like the clothes, were copies of some of the great designs of the 20s and 30s by Tiffany and Cartier.

Typical was a silver cigarette case decorated in red and black panels of Bakelite (I saw one exactly like it in an exhibition of costume jewellery of the twentieth century at the V&A a few years ago). She also favoured earrings in black, shiny Bakelite, ropes of cultivated pearls, and a vast number of brooches, some featuring sports cars and other streamlined designs. She had a collection of superior dress hangers in her wardrobe, covered in material to protect the garments, and she confided to me that she had won these as a prize in the egg and spoon race at the Royal Navy wives' club sports and social day at Whale Island in 1939. I saw her in action a couple of times when they managed to hold family days later in the war and she really was a dab hand at these novelty events. It was also something of a tradition that she would always win any 'prettiest ankles' contest she cared to enter.

On her parlour sideboard Grannie had a collection of what was then called 'German silver'. I wasn't much interested in the pretty little ornaments, but was riveted by the dagger in the silver scabbard. Gran could sense my fingers inching towards it even though she was on the other side of the room, cleaning the windows, with her back towards me.

"Put it down."

"Aw, Gran, I only wanted to look at it."

"Sure. And I am the Queen of the May."

"Is it a sword?"

"You know it isn't. Swords are much bigger. It's a dagger, a German officer's dress dagger from the last war. Your Uncle Alf brought it home from Germany for me."

"I expect he took it off some German he captured."

"I'm sure he did. Now stop fiddling about with it before you cut your fingers off. It's very, very sharp."

**********

Apart from the Lawrence family, we had other interesting neighbours. On our north side was brother and sister Percy and Kit Bodman. I think 'Pers' worked in Royal Clarence Victualling Yard, but Kit was definitely in showbiz. That's to say she had the cloakroom concession at the Forum cinema. As you passed through the foyer Kit would be sitting at her cloakroom counter, with a prominent saucer on the top for her tips.

The cloakroom was free (at Patrons' Own Risk) and Kit was paid no wages by the owners, her income being only what the patrons were prepared to spare. Except that she got a complimentary admission ticket for two once a week. Of course the job was a dead loss in the summer, but on a dirty night it was a goldmine. No Arab in the desert ever prayed more fervently for rain than Kit did for a wet Friday or Saturday, the busiest nights of the week. Popular opinion had it that it rained every day for the entire week that they showed that Hollywood hymn to British wartime pluck, Mrs Miniver, and Kit pocketed more money than the manager.

The war helped her in other ways, too. It was an offence to go out without your gas mask, especially for servicemen and women. But no-one wanted to sit nursing the cumbersome thing all through the movie, so Kit was very quick to offer to pop your respirator under the counter in the cloakroom. Her brother Percy, too, had his moment of local fame — but that was later.

On the other side of Grannie's was Mrs Gumbrell, who lived with her son. Like the Lawrences they had a decent conservatory built onto the rear of the house and were considered 'quite well-to-do.' Mrs G soon discovered I loved to read and lent me some of her son's childhood books, for which I will always be grateful.

I was preoccupied at this time looking forward to my sixth birthday. Apart from anything else it meant I would move into the top class at Newtown Infants at last. This was run by the fearsome Miss Tyler, who was infamous throughout the town of Gosport. God alone knew how old she was, but elderly people in the town that you met, say in the Co-op or Hayward's bakery, on hearing that you were at Newtown school would give a sharp intake of breath and try to freeze your blood....

"Newtown? Oh dear, you poor thing. You've got Miss Tyler? Oh, bad luck, son. She taught me — I know all about her."

She was formidably tall for a woman. Thin with grey hair and an English rose complexion (slightly faded and wrinkled), but with killer eyes behind her gold-rimmed specs. She favoured twin sets and pearls and I recall her usually in red with a straight skirt. The glint in her eye became quite pronounced when it came to punishing an unruly boy such as me.

"John Bull!" The call comes like a rifle shot across the classroom and I stiffen up as if hit by a bullet.

"Come here at once." Heart-sinking, I wriggle out from behind my desk, glance round at the (appalled) faces of the girls and boys in my class, and then I am on the scaffold.

"Turn round," and she spins me round to face the class. Then she leans over and raises the left leg of my short trousers and Slap! The palm of her hand slashes round and cuts across my thigh. I grit my teeth not to cry with the pain. Then eyes watering, face pink with shame, I'm sent stumbling back to my seat.

"Don't play about in my class again," orders the dragon.

As I waited for the magic birthday, Mum and I spent the spring sowing vegetable seeds in the garden. We dug the ground over, after a fashion, pulled up the weeds and sowed lettuce, carrots, peas, and spring onions, in neat little rows, at the end of which we put a twig with the seed packet over it to show what was in there. Mum insisted we sow some marigolds and other flowers, but I couldn't see much point in that.

"You can't eat flowers," I told her.

We had a couple of invasion scares at this time. As I came down to breakfast one morning I found Mum standing on the path with the front door open, peering about on the ground as if she'd lost something.

She called me out and pointed to some cigarette ends stamped out on the pavement. There were some dead matchsticks as well.

"I thought I heard something in the night," she said. "Men talking — and look at this. Somebody has been standing here, for some time, too. Looks like two or three men having a smoke." I could see she was worried.

"What's up, Mum?" I asked.

"Something woke me up. I thought I heard men marching, like soldiers," she told me. "Well there was somebody here anyway. You are not supposed to show a light in the blackout — the Germans can see the light of a match or a cigarette from thousands of feet up."

She mentioned the incident to the neighbours, but no-one else had heard anything so it remained a mystery.

Soon after, however, she woke me in the middle of the night.

"Did you hear anything?" she said, and she sounded worried. I hadn't heard a thing.

"It was the sound of marching feet again," she said. "Heavy boots tramping down Elmhurst Road. I looked out of the window but they must have gone. You sure you didn't hear it?" I shook my head.

"Do you think it was soldiers?" I asked her.

"To tell the truth I did think it was the Germans," said

Mum, her lip trembling, so I put my arms round her and gave her a hug.

"There would have been church bells ringing, Mum, if the Germans had come. You probably heard some of our soldiers getting ready to invade them."

Once again the neighbours had heard nothing and put Mum's fears down to 'nerves.' All the same, as she told my Grannie: "I can't help it, I've got a feeling that something bad is going to happen."

And how right she was. It was June now and in a few days time it would be June 14 — for Gosport and Portsmouth, another of the bad nights of the war.

By now most people had begun to regard the alert siren as the signal to put the kettle on to make a flask of tea before going to the shelter. Certainly when Moaning Minnie sounded that night, Mum was unusually slow to react. Or maybe our guns didn't open fire as promptly as usual, or maybe she didn't relish the trip down the garden to the back alley to get into Grannie's shelter.

I woke up as she gently shook me and told me to get my things on ready to go down. I don't think I heard any guns before the first terrifying whistle of a bomb came. There was a pretty loud explosion, followed quickly by another, and then another, getting closer and louder like a thunderstorm coming our way. As we got to the stairs, a colossal crash shook the house.

"God that was close," Mum shouted, winding her arms tight around me as she scrambled crabwise down the staircase. I heard the sound of breaking glass from the street. The air was suddenly full of choking smoke and dust. Mum shoved open the door of the cupboard under the stairs and pulled me inside with her. She slammed the door and switched on her torch. We could see swirling dust and not much else.

"Let's say a prayer together," she said, "Our Father...." and fixing my eyes solemnly on the timber steps of the stairs over my head, I joined in...."which art in Heaven...."

Suddenly the whole house leaps into the air. My chest is being crushed....I'm lying on the floor, can't get my breath. I scrabble for the door of the cupboard to find Mum already kicking desperately at it. I can't hear but I feel bricks and timber falling around us. Mum shines her torch around and dimly through the dust we can see wooden steps of the staircase still holding up, over our heads. We can't shift the door — we're both trapped by the rubble piled up outside.

We must have been screaming in panic at being buried alive —but deafened by the blast, we couldn't hear it.

It is worse for Mum — she's already been buried under a ton of rubble with her mother and brothers at the house in Queen's Road only a year before.

How long this goes on, I have no idea. After what seems like hours, Mum shakes me and points to the wooden frame of the cupboard. As I touch it I can feel someone banging steadily on the outside. Mum and me start hammering back, though no doubt our frightened screaming could be heard miles off.

Suddenly a beam of light shines around the edges of the door, a crowbar is bashed against it and we cower back against the wall. The door splinters and is prised away, the torch beam shines on us....

It shifts back to show us the grimy face of Uncle Alf, peering in. He hauls me smartly out and hands me over to someone else while he reaches back in for his sister. An air-raid warden holds up a Tilley lamp, Alf and the rescue team help us clamber over a heap of bricks, masonry and timber....once the back wall of the Bodmans' house next door. Some of the warden's team are digging in the rubble for Kit and Percy.

I was handed over to Uncle Bill, who took me to Grannie in the air-raid shelter. Somewhat to everyone's surprise I immediately climbed into a bunk and went straight off to sleep.

Next day I recall going to look at the damage. The bomb had exploded in the Bodmans' garden. The back of our house was wrecked, open to the weather, the proud French windows just a load of splintered wood and broken glass. But the Bodmans had the entire back of the house chopped off; the rubble sloping down into a huge crater. Earth had been flung everywhere.

Luckily none of us had more than cuts, mostly on our feet from the broken glass, and indeed the whole drama had ended on a note of near-farce when Mum and Alf, getting out gingerly over the rubble, came upon the spectre of a mud-covered Percy Bodman, crawling slowly out of the crater like some alien from a crashed spaceship. He had been asleep when the bomb exploded and the blast hurled him, bed and all, out of the house to slide on the collapsing brickwork into the hole. Like Mum and me, he was deafened by the blast and couldn't hear properly for days. Kit, sleeping at the other end of the house had managed to get down the stairs and out the front door unscathed.

None of our rooms was habitable. Next day the uncles went carefully upstairs to inspect and then helped Mum take a look around. To her horror she found her precious light oak dining table (with the greenish tinge) irreparably scarred by glass and debris. Nevertheless she refused to part with it and kept it as a war souvenir well into the 1960s.

The Gumbrells took me and Mum in as temporary lodgers. Grannie went to stay with her older daughter Auntie Gert on the Grange estate, practically on the airfield. I think we lived a sort of gypsy life for a week or two.

By now the officials at the town hall had become reasonably used to handling displaced persons, and providing emergency rations, loans and items lost in the bombing. They also recorded meticulously every claim for war damage compensation. This meant Mum and Grannie toiling over to some office in Portchester, not easy to get to, involving at least two buses, where they filled in the forms. This bit sticks in my mind because, since the uncles were back at work, it was easier to keep me off school and take me with them .

Eventually they got their money, after a very long wait. Incidentally, I never heard of anyone prepared to admit they got properly compensated for loss.

"I should have claimed twice as much as that for those curtains — but everything was at sixes and sevens and I had too much on my mind at the time," was Grannie's oft repeated moan to her intimates. Along with: "We've been bombed out three times, you know!"

Ever after, whenever chat turned to the days of the Blitz, she would produce this as calculated to top anything a neighbour could come up with. In fact, she and Grandpa and my uncles were bombed out of two houses, and Mum and me were bombed out of two homes, so as a family we could have claimed four bombings. But Grannie's conscience probably baulked at that, so she figured we were entitled to claim three. For God-fearing Gosport folk this was, and still is, an acceptable piece of logic.

Other logic was at work after the bomb. My playmates, Newtown Infants kids like Ronnie Moore, Wally Plummer and his cousins, the Ware family, knew that my birthday was on June 18. A couple of days after the raid a bunch of them came to see me at Mrs Gunmbrell's and were intercepted by Mum in the garden who was wondering what they wanted.

One of the girls, bolder than the others, naturally, blurted out: "Please Missus, is John going to have a party?"

"Party?"

"For his birthday...."

She looked at the expectant faces, a lesson in the resilience of children. These kids were lucky to be alive: they could have been killed, blinded or maimed. No doubt she took a deep breath, maybe even swallowed a sob or two....

"Party is it? Listen you lot, we haven't even got a roof over our heads, never mind parties. Come back next year and I'll see what I can do."

**********

As the tally of bomb damage began to mount, people became hardened to other's misfortune. As we walked about the rubble-strewn streets we got used to the sudden sight of a well-known landmark, perhaps the house of a friend, yesterday a neat terraced home and some mother's pride and joy, callously shattered overnight.

In the beginning, the brazen sight of the raw interior of someone's house, where yesterday there had been a decent, homely façade, was hard to take. Most people were shocked when confronted with an indecent display of someone's intimate bedroom furniture open to the sky, three parts of a room hanging onto a sagging floor half-way up the side of a terrace house. It gave a whole, hideous new meaning to the phrase semi-detached. I have never forgotten the horror I felt when for the first time I saw a better class of house torn apart like that. What really upset me was the sight of the porcelain lavatory pan, in what had once been a proud indoor bathroom, openly hanging from the middle of a wall, held up by what was left of the lead-pipe plumbing. To me it was dirty, shameful: had I been older I would probably have said obscene.

The authorities, slow to catch on, tended to leave damaged buildings on open display, until they realised what that was doing to morale. After that, they quickly moved in the boys with the long hooks for tearing down walls and timbers and the swinging iron ball for demolishing brickwork. And then the town began to have its scars reduced to bombed sites clinically cleared of rubble. In no time these were covered in weedy vegetation and criss-crossed by paths where people found they could take short cuts that didn't exist before. Very handy. Very adaptable, the Brits.

People didn't just get used to the misfortunes of others — the less-scrupulous even began to exploit them. Earlier it was all compassion. But human nature being what it is, there came the time when we started to see signs hung on deserted homes saying 'No looting.'

And that soon changed to 'Looters will be shot.' And eventually, on a bomb-shattered house in Avenue Road, someone went to the trouble of putting up a gibbet complete with a very lifelike corpse dangling from it — its face hideously contorted — and across the chest the sign 'I was a looter.'

Keeping thieves out of your damaged home was a big problem. The council or the ARP people  would send round a gang to put up a fence or nail planks across gaps in the walls, but after a big raid it took time to get around to everyone. Mum went back to the wreckage on the morning after our raid and found some light-fingered swine had lifted the green glass ring-holder from her dressing table, complete with her engagement ring and a couple of very nice dress rings.

This was too much for the gypsy in her soul to bear. She waited until a few neighbours were around, and went into ceremonial Romany mode. She mounted a pile of brick rubble, turned her gaze to the sky and held out both arms in supplication:

"Damn the man who stole my rings," she declared, head thrown back to gaze, black-browed, at the eternal sky overhead. "Damn him, I say. I, Nell Ferré, do place a solemn curse on the thief. May his fingers fester and drop off."

Then she seemed to go into a trance and had to be led away by a neighbour. "C'mon love, don't take on so. I'll make us a nice cup of tea."

A couple of days later, during the morning, one of the men clearing up the rubble approached Mum as she was collecting bits and pieces of furniture from the shattered living room.

"Ere Missus," he said, "I think these rings belong to you. I found them this morning." He held out the glass ring holder complete with rings. Mum took them from him and looked hard into his face.

"It was just over there — sitting on a pile of rubble," he muttered, trying to avoid her eyes.

"Yes," said Mum, "that was very good of you to get them for me. God bless you. By the way, how's that hand of yours?" He tried to shove his hand into his pocket, but she held on long enough to see the red sores and flaked skin all over his fingers.

"Oh," he said, "Just a bit sore, like." And he hurried away, guilty face flaring crimson.

I suffered in a similar way. I had a tin trunk where I kept my toys. The workmen had brought it out from the wreckage of the living room, where it had been kept in a cupboard under the dresser. The men had left it just outside in the rubble of the garden. I eagerly opened it up. Most the games and toys were OK. My beloved pre-war lead soldiers were all there. But where were my binoculars and my pair of handcuffs? I went off tearfully to complain to Mum.

"Never mind, son," she said, "the kids that took them won't get much luck, I'm sure."

A couple of weeks later, when we had moved home, I was playing with my school friend Ronnie Moore outside his house in Queen's Road, when a boy I didn't know came running by — handcuffed. I grabbed him and had a good look at the toy cuffs. They were mine all right: there was a distinctive scratch on the lock where I'd tried to open them with a screwdriver instead of using the catch.

"Where d'ya get these?"

"They're my brother's."

A boy about my age came up, just as I took the cuffs off.

"Wossup?"

"These 'andcuffs are mine. Swiped from our bombed house. I'm takin' 'em back see? And what 'ave you done with my binoculars?"

"Dunno nuffink about that," the older brother said. Then, realising he'd as good as admitted knowing about the toy handcuffs, he pulled the other kid away and they ran off down the road. For weeks I went about staring suspiciously at any kid who might be concealing my binoculars, but I never did get them back. Looters deserve to be shot.

In a strange twist of fate David Lawrence, teenage fireman in the Blitz on Gosport, later photographed the exploding of the first atomic bomb on the Japanese city of Hiroshima in 1945. David served in the Pacific as a Royal Navy cameraman and this was his last special mission. He and I often worked together when I became a cub reporter on the Portsmouth Evening News. Naturally, when I duly moved to Fleet Street, I ordered pictures from him whenever we needed one from Gosport. Later yet, when I edited a company newspaper for Cyanamid, the American pharmaceutical multinational with UK headquarters in Gosport, I again had the pleasure of working with David. And in all that time he never said a word about his Hiroshima shoot. The secret came out when a relative revealed it at his funeral in 2005. David was a sensitive chap and I imagine he kept his mouth shut because, like me, he found the story too ironic for words.

David Lawrence doubling as a young Blitz fireman

# Chapter Seven
# Shilooties of the Home Front

We finally found a new home towards the end of June 1941. It wasn't easy to get a place to rent with so many families suddenly being made homeless. In any case, the rapid expansion of the navy, and the calling up of soldiers, sailors and airmen, not to mention the growth of women's services, had already put a huge strain on accommodation in and around Portsmouth and Gosport.

However, Uncle Alf had the bright idea of us all sharing a larger place. So Mum and me joined Grannie and Grandpa, Alf and Bill, in renting a five-bedroom house at 40 Peel Road, formerly the home of a Mayor of Gosport, Councillor C E Davis, and it was posh enough to have a name — 'Rownhams', after a village near Southampton.

Grannie was fond of telling her pals these interesting snippets, along with mentioning as often as possible that the house had central heating, a bathroom with hot and cold water, two indoor lavatories, and a very modern 1930s kitchen with a gas cooker. As for me, I loved that house and its garden. I still regard the wartime years I spent there as the best thing that ever happened to me.

Though an only child, I had company all the time: adults from whom to learn about life. They introduced me to newspapers and, on top of that, the place was always full of books and magazines. It is where I began to appreciate the full meaning of the magic word 'home.'

It was a tall building, imposing to people used to narrow, rather dwarfish, terrace houses, and it fronted on to Peel Road with two entrances. The one on the north side bore the name Rownhams, and led across a tiled patio, surrounded by hydrangeas, to the front door set at right angles inside a deep porch. The other gate, labelled 'Trademen's entrance', opened onto a path leading, via a trelliswork screen with a gate, to the back door and a substantial brick-built outhouse known as the 'washhouse' because it contained a coal-fired boiler for doing the washing (His Worship the Mayor probably had a housekeeper to do that). The wide garden ran down to three tall lime trees in front of a brick wall topped with broken glass to keep out intruders from Avenue Road. Around the overgrown lawn were several apple trees, a useful pear tree and a quince espalier-ed against the back of the washhouse.

A fence ran along the Peel Road frontage, with a privet hedge planted behind, and behind that was the imposing, bay-windowed, brick façade of the house. 'Rownhams' is still there and it doesn't look all that different today except the fence has been replaced by a rather nice low wall, and the porch to the front door has been remodelled and filled in to protect callers from the rain.

The front door opened onto a tiled hall, hexagonal in shape with, moving clockwise, the broad staircase, beneath which was hidden a lavatory with one of those little windows of 'bubble' glass to make it opaque. Next came the 'front' room with a big bay window overlooking Peel Road, which for a while we used simply as a place to store our overflow of furniture; then a large walk-in pantry, Grannie's favourite place. It contained a meat safe, a milk cooler, and stacks of shelving to store bottled fruits, jams and chutneys — a real-old style cook's domain. Presumably the mayor had kept a cook, or maybe a parlour maid.

People of quite humble means expected to get a little help around the house in the Thirties. Working-class women, like my Grannie, would be quite likely to have a skivvy, a girl of say 14 or 15, usually from a large family that needed help. Grannie would take the girl in, feed and clothe her, and give her a shilling or two pocket money in return for her lighting the fires in the morning, dusting, cleaning, washing and ironing, preparing veg and answering the door. The girl would stay for up to a year, until old enough to be of use in the labour market, say as a shop assistant. The male equivalent was the van boy, or butcher's delivery boy, a cheerful breed of brat that generally made himself useful in the community. Along with the skivvies, of course, they disappeared at the start of World War II never to return, much to the deep regret of Grannie and her contemporaries.

Next on our clockwise tour was the kitchen, the warm, beating heart of the home.

The centrepiece was the stove, a versatile creature that consumed coal or coke and warmed every part of the house via the large-bore water pipes and radiators fed from tanks in the attic. In those bitter, wartime winters this was treated like a god, to be worshipped and glorified.

There was a deep butler sink, with hot water on tap, a gas cooker, and a long, scrubbed table where all food preparation was done. There was ample shelving and overhead racks, for drying clothes or for curing a ham, which could be raised or lowered by a rope running through a pulley set in the ceiling.

Most of our meals were taken in the kitchen, but on Sundays or special celebrations we dined in the proper dining room next door which, in fact, we treated most of the time as our living room. It was where we listened to the wireless, or played cards or games.

I've been lucky to be happy in most of the homes I've had but this, to me, was truly exceptional. My grandfather died in that house, the only one I have ever lived in that saw birth or death. For me this underlines the difference between my family's past and the awkward present. Few people are born — or die — at home these days, which I think denigrates the 'feel' we have for our houses, makes them seem disposable, underlining how temporary is our stay here.

Before the move, my uncles, aided by neighbours, dug out Grannie's Anderson shelter and Mum was persuaded to get a new one for us. These shelters consisted of two sets of corrugated sidepieces which formed an arched, rounded roof, where they were bolted together. The uncles dug deep new footings in the earth, and this time set the sidewalls in concrete to a depth of 18 inches, so that we had a double-length shelter for us all. Then they fitted the corrugated iron front and end pieces, covered the whole thing with sandbags and finally covered that all over with turf. And when they fitted the entrance door they added a four-foot high brick wall at the front as an anti-blast barrier. We felt we were going to be safe from anything other than a direct hit from a high-explosive bomb.

In the absence of my father at sea, the man we looked to as head of the family was Uncle Alf — my mother's older brother. He was the same age as the year, in other words in 1941 he was 41. He had been called up in 1918 and caught the end of WWI in the trenches. Like all veterans of that war that I have met, he never spoke about the fighting. It was as if all old soldiers from that war had signed a sort of unofficial don't-go-there agreement best summed up in a song they adapted from an old music hall hit — 'From this great big world of ours, you've chosen me....'

And when they ask us
And they're certainly going to ask us
Why we didn't win the bleedin' Croix de Guerre
Oh we'll never tell them
Oh we'll never tell them
There was a front — but damned if we knew where.

Like my other uncles on my father's side of the family — two of whom were Old Contemptibles (it means they were regular soldiers, in from the start in 1914 and comes from the Kaiser's haughty dismissal of 'England's contemptible little army') — they would happily talk about their training in Wiltshire or picking up ma'm'selles in ooh-la-la Paree, but as for the bombs and bullets, or the blood and guts, or the gassed and blinded, that sort of talk was only to be shared with someone who was there.

Uncle Alf told us many tales, especially of his time after the Armistice when he was billeted in a big house along the Rhine, and about the Germans, for whom he had the greatest respect. Especially the ordinary working people, men and women who, like him, wanted to live in a better world.

But back in civvy street Uncle Alf had a hard time. He had no trade — and there was no work for unskilled hands. He would have done anything. In the end, after years of unemployment, he was taken on by the water company as a navvy. His bosses repeatedly promised him promotion to keep a clever and hard-working man on board, but by 1939 it hadn't happened. When the raids began, he and his gang mended bombed pipes, often working all night, soaking wet, in a different kind of trench warfare. Their job was to keep the water supply going for the firefighters and, maybe more importantly, making sure that smashed sewers never polluted the drinking supply.

Before the war, Authority's big fear was that bombing would cause a plague of cholera in towns and cities, bringing panic and a general breakdown of the system; the sort of horror predicted by the novelist Nevil Shute in his 1939 book What Happened to the Corbetts — about a young professional man and his wife settling into their first home in Southampton. Without warning, enemy planes bomb the city night after night, easily evading ineffective fighter aircraft and anti-aircraft guns. Civil organisation quickly breaks down, water supplies are contaminated and people are soon dying like flies from cholera.

Thank God the plague never happened, even in the worst of the London Blitz, thanks to the skill and dedication of the men and women in the municipal water companies who worked until they dropped to keep fresh water coming.

That, and the know-how of the civil servants who organised food rationing so that no-one went hungry, was the great, forgotten contribution that civilians made to the war effort. Such often-maligned people kept the country running without a serious hitch for nearly six years. My Uncle Alf deserved a medal, though I doubt he'd have taken it, if offered. Ten Woodbines and a pint of old and mild, maybe.

Alf's younger brother, Uncle Bill, was a happy-go-lucky Dockyard Matey, whose role was to keep us cheerful, which he did by bashing out songs on the piano or his banjo-mandolin. He got his name in the Portsmouth Evening News twice: once for being found with his crony Ron drunk and asleep in someone else's air-raid shelter, and later for trapping a bloke who stole cash from the Clarence Yard safe.

Grandpa, the bookie's runner (retired) was....well, just Grandpa. His feet were too bad to enable him to play a major role against Hitler, though he joined up as a fire-watcher and was given an armband to wear. The rest of the family joked that the only fire he was likely to watch was the one in the grate at the Albert, the pub in Queen's Road where he used to play dominoes. This pub was kept by Old Arfield, a veteran of the trenches in the Great War, who had been gassed at Ypres and whose lungs had never properly recovered. In winter he was prone to terrible bouts of coughing from which he swore that only a dose of whisky brought any relief, apart from sucking coal-black chunks of Spanish liquorice that my grandmother kept him supplied with from a secret source of her own.

With Grannie and Grandpa as child minders at home, my mother joined Auntie Gert and her oldest girl Freda in PH — Priddy's Hard, the Royal Navy's munitions yard on the Gosport side of the harbour, staffed almost entirely by women. All I knew was that they used to check that the shells supplied by arms factories would fit in the guns. I had no idea how they did this, but imagined it was similar to chipping rust off cannonballs like they did in Nelson's navy to make them fly true.

I know they used to sing a lot. One ditty, to the tune of 'What a Friend We Have in Jesus,' ran:

"No more going to the matron
No more cutting off our hair
You can tell the bloody matron
To stick her scissors....on the shelf."

Or, at least, that was the version they sang in front of us kids. Presumably long hair was regarded as a safety hazard when working with explosives.

I was allowed to go as far as St George's Barracks in Spring Garden Lane to meet Mum coming home from work. She wore a shabby, navy blue raincoat and a headscarf, called a 'turban', from under which peeped a few fair curls and her striking blue eyes. As a treat she sometimes gave me a cream bun saved from her canteen lunch.

The one who really ran things, though, was Grannie. To keep us all fed, warm and healthy in wartime meant she and women like her had to develop a shell of indomitable matriarchy. Grannie had borne five children of her own, the youngest of whom, Edie, had died as a little girl. And even after that, she also took in two more children just in their teens, Charlie and Dolly, after their parents were drowned. She had brought her family safely through World War I, the Great War, as they all called it, which she often described as a sort of rehearsal for the real one 20 years later.

Because my mother went to work for most of the war, you could say it was Grannie who brought me up: in fact she was a major influence of my life. She introduced me to books, helped me with the longer words in the newspapers, and taught me to cook. Every time I wash vegetables, or make pastry, or fry fish in a pan, I see her worn fingers moving deftly at the task. I hear her instructing me: "Keep it moving, keep it turning."

I was born in her house at 123 Queen's Road, and I stayed with her and Grandpa when Mum was in hospital. They looked after me whenever she had a job. When she went to PH and worked long wartime hours, this became pretty much the norm.

Grannie had a pretty regular meals routine. Sunday: ideally roast beef, an H-bone if available but, with rationing and shortages, whatever 'meat' we could get: sometimes we'd be lucky enough to get what we hoped was a rabbit. Mondays: cold meat left over from Sunday, chips, pickle, or fresh veg. Tuesday: stew, mostly veg and dumplings to eke out the meat ration. Wednesday: sausages, a bit of liver or kidneys, and mashed spuds. Thursday: meat pie (don't ask) and veg such as swede or turnip. Friday: always fish, as befitted a good Anglo Catholic family. Boiled, steamed, grilled or fried, it was unrationed and there was always something available.

Grandpa's betting customers among the fishermen down on the waterfront would often offer him a bucketful of 'scraps' which he would fetch home. You could dine on the same thing years later in pretentious restaurants, only they covered it with batter and called it 'scampi.'

The main meal of the day was taken early in the evening, except on Saturdays when we all had our dinner around one o'clock, and on Sunday when we sat down after the 'boys' came back from the Albert at two. Weekdays I had my dinner at school, wholesome no doubt, but mass cooking at its deadliest. The smell of over-cooked cabbage permanently hung around the classrooms and anyway I could afford to be choosy because later I was going to share whatever Grannie had cooked the family for my supper.

My comic used to come on Tuesdays: the Beano and the Dandy were published on alternate weeks to save paper.

"Eat your stew. You can read your comic later," says Gran. I had it propped up in front of me. Lord Snooty and his pals had uncovered a German spy at Bunkerton Castle....

A tantalising whiff of stew, with just a hint of something tangy....as a dish is waved over me.

"What's it got in it, Gran? Something smells different...."

"It's in the juiper" she says, meaning the gravy. "Just a touch of curry powder on the meat."

She didn't ask whether I liked it or not. But then, I suppose, she saw me lick the plate clean.

I don't think I have ever cooked an Irish stew since without putting a spoonful of curry paste in the gravy.

**\*\*\*\*\*\*\*\*\*\***

Over all this domestic life hung the war....and the spectre of the Luftwaffe bombing raids. Uncle Alf was called out night after night to repair broken water mains. Stories of the horrors of the air raids went from mouth to mouth:

"The 'ole family was sitting upright round the kitchen table, just like they was about to 'ave their dinner. Not a mark on any of 'em — but they was all stark naked. The blast had tore off all their clothes. And they was all stone dead."

It happened over at — Hardway, or Fareham, or Cosham. It was always somewhere a bit farther off. And clearly based on truth somewhere:

Three girls were walking home from the pictures when the siren went. A policeman stopped them and ordered them to go into the air-raid shelter on the corner....one of them ducked away from him and ran off home. The other two went into the shelter....and were killed along with the others in there when it took a direct hit.

And it wasn't always about air-raids, or far-off battles in the Med. That autumn we heard about an Isle of Wight paddle steamer, possibly the Portsdown, that hit a mine in the Solent while on passage from Portsmouth to Ryde — with the loss of many passengers (apparently no-one counted them or checked names when they boarded.)

\*\*\*\*\*\*\*\*\*\*

I've mentioned earlier the plan to drive a tunnel under Portsmouth harbour with the idea of linking Gosport to Portsmouth by a rail shuttle — the Kearney tube, brainchild of an enterprising American engineer, Chalmers Kearney, who reckoned it would cost £400,000 all up. In 1939 Gosport Council set up a committee to consider the scheme. Portsmouth City Council, for their part, decided to keep an eye on a similar Kearney scheme already being considered in North and South Shields, and there the matter rested.

But when the heavy night raids began at the end of 1940, Kearney suggested the tunnel could be used as a deep shelter.

In a letter to the Mayor of Gosport, Alderman J R Gregson, dated August 7 1941, Kearney promised:

"I can obtain the money from America and there is no coercion on the Government to provide for the expenditure. There is no cost whatever to the Corporations. Both Local Authorities are allowed to have the tunnel and existing works handed over free of cost after the war to operate a Railway there if they so desire, but otherwise the tunnel and works to become the property of the original Donors."

The matter was put to the vote at a special meeting of Gosport Borough Council on August 11 when the proposition was defeated 17 votes to 4.

**********

Our family air raid shelter was in use almost as soon as we moved in to Peel Road. By now the family's air defence and survival technique was much better organised. Uncle Alf had rigged up a little spirit lamp, run on methylated spirits, as emergency lighting and everyone was equipped with a torch. Mine constantly needed a new battery because I'd use it for reading at night under the bedclothes. Grannie had a superior heavy-duty Royal Navy issue torch (identifiable like so many items in Gosport homes by the broad arrow government mark stamped upon it to show it was stolen from the Crown). Uncle Alf had his water company bullseye lantern, and the rest of us had bicycle lamps.

There were four comfortable, if narrow bunks, two each side, and a small cross-bunk across the end where they usually put me. There were also a couple of folding chairs in the middle, and storage drawers under the bunks, with tinned food and other emergency rations, including a bottle of rum, a pick and a couple of shovels in case of another digging out job (God forbid).

When Moaning Minnie got us out of bed we would get to the shelter as quickly as possible. In earlier days, when we were told that the German pilots could see the light of a flaring match at 3,000 feet, we used to stumble about in the dark. In practice we found the sky well lit by searchlight beams and gun flashes, not to mention the occasional illumination of a burning house. In any case the family view was that the shaded beam of a torch was worth risking, better than a broken ankle or being garotted by the clothes line.

There was an unseemly scramble to squeeze between the blast wall and at the same time undo the hasp on the entrance door, then down three wooden steps inside. Grannie used to go first, flick open the door and push me in, followed by Mum and Grandpa. My uncles, Alf and Bill, or 'the boys', as Gran called them, would usually stand 'up top' wearing their tin hats, their work-issued steel helmets, watching the show until the first bomb fell, when they would dive into the dugout.

Some nights I managed to wriggle unnoticed into a position close to the doorway from where I could see the night sky, the clouds scudding across lit by the moon, or the probing searchlight beams. A full moon could mean a quieter night. At the start people used to call it 'the bomber's moon' because it showed up the target, but by now our fighter pilots, guided by radar, could get within seeing range of the bomber and shoot it down. By now the Germans were wary of dangerous moonlight and tended to avoid it.

My abiding picture of Uncle Alf is of his tall, helmeted figure, standing steady on watch, against a backdrop of stars and searchlight beams, accompanied by far-off gunfire and the occasional crunch of a bomb. He was always fully dressed ready for the callout message (delivered by a warden) to lead his gang out to fix a damaged main. In the heavier raids, he was rarely disappointed.

One of these nights came early in the autumn, I seem to recall that darkness hadn't long fallen when we hurried down into the shelter. Usually we had a sort of warning period when we could hear bombs falling some way off — over Pompey maybe. But this night we seemed to be in the thick of it right from the start, and our anti-aircraft guns were making my ears hurt.

Mum put my pillow on top of my head and held the ends down over my ears to muffle the noise. It worked.... up to a point. A messenger came to get Uncle Alf early on and, without him around, the raid always got worse somehow.

The screaming-whistle of a bomb seemed to be right overhead. We ducked and stopped breathing until the bang came.

Grannie said: "Oh, no. Don't say we're going to be bombed out again. We've only just got straight from the last lot."

Grandpa put his arm round her: "With all the practice you've had....you'll take it in your stride, Allie. Don't worry, he'll be all right. Alf knows how to keep his head down."

Next day we heard that the bombs had hit houses in the Leesland area, a short walk away, people had been killed and there were a lot of casualties. Several houses were wrecked.

The borough's official figures list those killed on September 20 1941 as Mrs Ada Brown (formerly Freebury) aged 37, her 14-month-old daughter Vera and 15-year-old son Donald Freebury, at 46 Leesland Road. Across the road Joyce Ethel Glover ( 21), died at number 83, as did her neighbours at number 85, Emma Elizabeth Seabrook (66), and her husband, Ernest Edward (64), who died at the War Memorial Hospital from his bomb injuries.

\*\*\*\*\*\*\*\*\*\*

People used to talk about the 'dark days of 1940 to 1942 when Britain stood alone.' To us the phrase meant long, long winter evenings when the family, often including my cousins, played cards or board games, dominoes, draughts, ludo, and snakes and ladders.

I particularly loved a card game called Silhouettes, which I pronounced 'Shilooties'. The name caught on and all the family took to calling it Shilooties. It was based on the blackout, and each card carried the shadow of something topical — an air-raid warden, a tank, a barrage balloon and so on. Otherwise it was played similar to Happy Families: you had to collect sets of cards belonging to the same family or group.

Going out was limited by the need to stay near the shelter. But as the raids eased, Mum or Grannie would take me to some amateur show put on to raise money for some wartime cause.

All kinds of events were offered at the Shakespeare Hall in Queen's Road, and at the Vine pub in Stoke Road, which had a hall at the back. I remember a typical concert all the family went to at the Vine when my cousin Jimmy, in his teens, played the MC dressed as an overgrown schoolboy in short trousers, striped tie and minute school cap. We greeted him with jeers and boos whenever he stepped out from between the curtains to introduce an act....one of which was his younger sister Edna, who amazed us all by twisting her body about alarmingly as 'Exotic Edena... direct from Arabia.'

I remember Auntie Gert, her mother, muttering: "Double-jointed she may be, but I'm the one who'll have to put her head back on the right way round."

\*\*\*\*\*\*\*\*\*\*

In the autumn of 1941 there was a great deal of satisfaction in looking ahead to Christmas. December 25 was due to fall on a Thursday — the optimum day of the week for working folk. It meant no work on the two bank holidays, Christmas Day and Boxing Day, plus more time off on the Saturday and the Sunday, even though Saturday morning was usually a working day. The general feeling was: "After what we've been through this year we bloody well deserve four days!"

On that first wartime Christmas back in 1939 we had cheered the exploits of our cruisers, Ajax, Essex, Exeter and Cumberland in forcing the feared German battleship Graf Spee into Montevideo Harbour where she finally scuttled herself, and her commander blew his brains out.

In fact the British celebrated all six Christmases of the war with a fervour that has never been matched since. Most families had sons, daughters or husbands missing from the feast because they were on active service. And civvy families might have had someone on ARP duties, in the Home Guard, or on duty in hospital, 'doing their bit.'

Many, of course, had lost relatives in the bombing, or fighting abroad. And even if you did have everyone at home, you were conscious that this year it might be the last time. It made Christmas poignantly special....and, of course, the churches were full.

To finance our great annual feast Grannie and Mum paid into a year-round Christmas Club every week, probably about half-a-crown (12p) each.

"How much will you have by Christmas, Mum?" I remember asking.

"About a week's pay....and whatever we've got to come from the Co-op divi."

I knew all about the Co-op divi because it was dinned into me by Mum and Grannie that when I did my 'messages' — their word for shopping errands — I had to be able to give the Co-op shop assistant the correct dividend number, so that every penny spent went on the total. If you doubt that, I can tell you now that the number was 27814.

We were members of the Portsea Island Mutual Co-operative, PIMCO, and I recall that the divi was typically about eightpence in the pound, a not terribly impressive three percent. As the usual family spend would have been about £3 a week, it meant the Christmas divi payout was worth about £5.

"Huh, that's pretty miserable," Uncle Bill would say, thinking in terms of how many pints of bitter that represented — at sixpence a pint, say 200, which was not bad, but then he was a bit greedy over his beer. And Grandpa, his mind turning to thoughts of a bit of extra baccy, would smile tolerantly.

The women, who regarded all males as feckless idiots totally incapable of handling money, would roll their eyes and mentally work out how far £15 would go in extra groceries as well as drink.

Apart from the joy of opening the doors of the Advent calendar each morning, what kicked off the season for kids was the Christmas shopping trip 'over the water'. Shops like the Landport Drapery Bazaar and the big Co-op department store in Fratton Road always featured a Santa's Grotto (even after the shops were bombed to bits early in 1941 and reduced to welcoming us to makeshift stores that were little more than huts). My contemporaries still talk about the Christmas grotto at the Co-op that featured a submarine trip under the harbour — "You could see the fishes swimming by through the portholes along the sub's hull, you know, I can see it now....it was magic!"

The next step was making the puddings. Grannie used to make at least eight, in individual basins boiled for hours in a big pot with a broad arrow on the side, indicating that it had at one time belonged to His Majesty King George, or possible Her Majesty Queen Victoria — and which Grandpa never failed to describe as 'big enough to cook a missionary in.'

The wartime white-ish National flour was sieved to within an inch of its life before the marge and lard went in, then the spices and essences and whatever was available in the way of dried fruit, currants, sultanas, raisins (funny, whatever fruit was missing, there always seemed to be plenty of raisins around — I didn't like them much). Then there was candied peel of oranges and lemons, and spices that I imagined came from some eastern market as illustrated in my book of the Arabian Nights stories. The mix was topped off by the addition of a full quart of stout.... and the aroma alone was strong enough to fuddle the wits of a dray horse.

Of course I lent a hand, on the understanding I would be allowed to lick the bowl out when the mixture had been spooned into the basins.

The stirring was done with due ceremony, in Church of England homes on the Sunday before Advent, known as 'Stir up' Sunday, because that's how the Collect for the day began in the Book of Common Prayer ('Stir up, we beseech thee O Lord, the wills of thy faithful people'). Everyone in the family took part. Local papers in navy ports still carry a pre-Christmas picture of a ship's company stirring theirs — with the blade of an oar.

Grannie divided her mixture into eight basins, greaseproof paper was tied over the top, topped by a pudding cloth, and the hours of boiling began. The house filled with a beguiling aroma of spice and warm stout....I had to go out because I couldn't stand it.

Presents were already being wrapped, labelled and stowed away. The stark reality of war was all around us, but me and my pals still half-believed Father Christmas would somehow, if not exactly come down the chimney, nevertheless drop in to deliver the gifts, because we wanted to believe it. Our family had a tradition of going to the pub on Christmas Eve. The Anglican church did not introduce Midnight Mass until well after the war, preferring its Watch Night service on New Year's Eve, until it realised it was losing out to the Roman Catholics and changed, to keep the audience so to speak.

"Hip, hip hooray, it's Christmas Eve today," sang the parrot, a character in one of my story books. And I was puzzled.

"Eve just means the day before, whatever it is," Grannie tries to explain, "nothing to do with 'evening', that's different altogether."

"What about Hallow'een then? That 'een' has got to be short for evening, hasn't it?"

This is too much for Grannie.

"Look, Christmas Eve starts when you have your breakfast...so eat up your egg and enjoy," she declares. "We've got lots to do before we hang up our stockings."

My preparations mostly involved blackleading the stove, chopping wood and kindling, and filling scuttles from the coal-hole. Then there was general tidying up at the direction of Grandpa, until she got fed up with us both and packed us off out on some errand, which somehow usually involved us visiting the Albert during the lunchtime licensed hours.

The main aim was to tire me out so that I wouldn't wake them too early next day. So I was allowed to stay up a bit later, and even went out into the garden in the dark to see the stars.

Starlight, especially early in the evening before the moon came up over the trees, seemed to have a special magic about it, a cool, deep atmosphere of quiet, sort of suspended in the sky....and, to my constant surprise, this continues still to be the case every Christmas Eve.

"Jerry seems to be leaving us alone again this year," said Uncle Alf, coming out to join Mum and me on Christmas Eve 1941.

"Maybe they're superstitious," suggested my mother.

"Yeah. They used to make a big thing out of Christmas Eve, before Hitler took over," he said. He was gazing up at the night sky. Then he started softly whistling....and Mum quietly sang....

"Silent night, Holy night....all is calm, all is bright,
Round yon Virgin mother and child,
Holy infant so tender and mild,
Sleep in Heavenly peace, Sle-ep in Heavenly peace."

**********

I hung up my stocking, as did the rest of the family, from the mantelpiece over the fire. To please me, Uncle Bill had carefully selected the most darned sock he possessed....to match the illustration in the Christmas issue of the Dandy, which he passed around so that everyone could compare his stocking with Korky the Cat's.

Usually I fell asleep as soon as my head touched the pillow....but whenever I woke I instantly knew it was Christmas — but what time? Then I'd carefully, hopefully, reach down with one foot under the bedclothes to see if 'Santa had been.' Eventually there it was: the thrill of feeling a lumpy bag at the end of my bed....and of the grey, dawn filtering through the heavy blackout curtains. Lying there, impatient, I'd call out to Mum:

"Can I look at my presents?"

A hoarse whisper from her room: "Be quiet. You can see what's in your stocking. Anything else must wait till we start getting up."

The stocking....little novelties, a tin whistle or a Kazoo, maybe a rubber dagger....a spud gun, blackface soap, chocolate money, or indoor fireworks and some sticks of Plasticine, a shiny red apple, a small orange....

Here's an actual list (as far as memory serves) of the presents from those wartime Christmases (1941-43): a toy Tommy gun with realistic sound effects, a 2ft wingspan bomber, a 'Sherlock Holmes' detective outfit, a clockwork ambulance, a Monopoly set, a Rupert annual, a book of boys' stories, Siberian Gold by Theodore Acland Harper (it's here on my desk now....'from Auntie Gert and Uncle Jim, Christmas 1942'), and, of course, the card game called Silhouettes.

Mum used to leave little dishes of sweets and dried fruits, such as figs and dates, for people to snack on during the morning, which we all did even at the risk of spoiling our appetites for the big meal of the year. For people used to going hungry, it was a non-problem.

The goose or the turkey was well-stuffed, usually with a mixture that included mashed chestnuts. Mum and Grannie worked on the spuds to be roasted, the sprouts to be boiled (but not for too long), carrots (both boiled and roasted), redcurrant jelly, cranberry sauce, and a superlative gravy which contained a glass of sherry. The uncles busied about with wood and coal for the fires, including a large basket of Yule logs. Grandpa took me to Christ Church and I was allowed to take one of my smaller presents to show off, obviously not a book.

The family sat down around Grannie's big table in the dining room some time after 1pm. At a signal give by Grannie, Uncle Alf poured everyone a glass of sherry for an appetiser, as if the scents filling the air from the kitchen were not making us ravenous already.

"Can I have a drop of sherry, too?" I ask Mum.

"You can have a sip....but why don't you wait until later and have a small glass of port with your pudding? You can have one or the other....not both."

"I'll wait for the port wine then." Except I probably call it 'pork wine' — this being due to a mis-association of ideas among me and my younger cousins. Working-class British families rarely touched wine in those days....except for token sherries and ports at festive occasions, hence the connection in our minds with pork.

Uncle Bill invites me to pull a cracker with him, and then we're all at it amid the crackle of snapping gunpowder, a spilling out of gaudy rings and brooches and paper hats, which we all put on, and mottoes and conundrums which are solemnly read out....to loud groans at the bad puns, which try as you might you will never be able to forget:

"Why was the chicken wrong to cross the road? — Because it is a foul (fowl) proceeding."

The turkey is borne proudly in. Grandpa is asked to carve, but he graciously turns to his elder son and offers him the honour — which he has done each year since 1939 — to give the boy his chance of family responsibility. The main course is dealt with more or less silently, not to say reverently. But general discussion breaks out again, becoming merrier as more drinks are poured, ale for the men and wine cordials for the ladies.

Then, as in a scene from Dickens's A Christmas Carol, Grannie carries in the pudding in great triumph and ceremony, dark, rich, reeking of the spices of Araby, topped with a sprig of English holly and ablaze with bright blue flames of blazing rum. The room, shadowed by the leaden light of the winter afternoon, is warm and glowing from the living fire, which flickers across the faces of the family making their eyes shine....that's how I remember them as they raise their glasses of ruby wine — "Merry Christmas Everyone."

\*\*\*\*\*\*\*\*\*\*

Later Uncle Alf and Uncle Bill light up their Christmas cigars, Wills Whiffs or a rare Punch panatela. Grandpa gets his pipe going — and Grannie directs him to sit by the fire. His tobacco, some dreadful navy shag brought by a sailor home from sea, is very strong and she hopes the smoke will go up the chimney and give the curtains and furnishings a break.

"Right you are, Allie," he says happy enough to escape to his armchair. He winks at me and I slip down from the table to sit at his feet....and get a secret sip of wine. It's three o'clock. Uncle Alf has switched on the radio and we hear the chimes of Big Ben ring out over battered London, and all over the Empire-on-which-the-sun-never-sets....

"Ladies and Gentlemen....His Majesty the King:"

"My very good wishes to you all...." his voice is a little querulous, but the stammer of his earlier years is almost gone. His message is simple: "We have stood alone. We have shown we can take it. Now we are no longer alone. Our American cousins in the West have once more joined us in the fight against tyranny. They have raised the standard to fight alongside the land of their forebears...." Or words to that noble effect.

The faces round the table, foolish grins wiped away, have a steady sober look, and a proud lift of the chin. No we are not alone any more....maybe we can think about dishing it out now....and with that happy, bloody-minded thought, we all drift off to sleep.

**\*\*\*\*\*\*\*\*\*\***

In the evening the whole family gathers round the table to play Monopoly. The set is a wartime production, with cardboard and wood counters for the players instead of the silver ones from 'pre war'. My favourite is the battleship, because of Dad somewhere at sea.

"I expect he's having a lovely time," Uncle Bill tells me. "Probably lying on some warm beach on a tropical island."

"I do hope so," says Mum putting her brother in his place. He hurriedly starts dealing the property cards in their coloured sets, as we are going to play the 'short' version of the game. I am fascinated by the 'scrip,' beautifully printed notes from £1 up to the opulent £500s. I make a secret resolve to try to copy some — the tens would be easier, as they are in black and white. We all arrange our property cards by colour and later we will start bargaining with each other to acquire whole sets and start building houses.

We throw the dice, rejoice as we swing past GO and collect £200, and groan when we land on Income Tax and have to pay £100 back to Uncle Alf, who always take the role of Banker. A very honest and strict Banker (apart from slipping me the odd £500 in my change when no-one is looking). With all these adults to play with I am more advanced at the game than my contemporaries, though my weakness is that whatever the other players are doing in the property market, my sole aim is to acquire the Picadilly-Coventry Street-Leicester Square trio because yellow happens to be my favourite colour.

You know of a better way to play Monopoly? Tonight I find it surprisingly easy to get the set and soon my eyelids droop and I'm asleep before someone kindly carries me up the wooden hill to bed.

**********

In the worst days of the Battle of the Atlantic we often were hungry as key foods became scarce. Grannie's Christmas puddings would be sweetened with honey instead of sugar, and she made trifles with tins of 'pineapple' that were really chunks of swede in fruit juice, a device that was officially adopted by Lord Woolton's Ministry of Food in their regular bulletins and newspaper ads advising people how to improvise.

"Yeuk," I hear you say , "I couldn't eat that." Don't fret, neither did we.

Wartime shortages and 'making do' meant that people suffered from trivial, but annoying little diet-deficiency illnesses or skin conditions. Thus there was the Christmas of the Whitlows when both my mother and grandmother developed painful sores on their fingers. Cooking was obviously out of the question so my uncles, assisted by me and Grandpa, courageously made all the mince pies, cakes and puddings. The puddings came out gritty and inedible, the pies rock hard. Uncle Bill carelessly knocked one off the kitchen table. It fell on his ankle. He always blamed that mince pie for the limp that marked his progress for the rest of his life. Another war wound to go with the swastika scar on his forehead from being buried alive by the bomb in Queen's Road.

One bad year, probably Christmas 1942, we were threatened by a meat shortage. Turkeys, geese, ducks, even chicken, might all have vanished off the face of the earth. Any suggestion that Mr Silk, the butcher, could possibly take an order for a Christmas bird was met with a brittle laugh:

"Christmas bird is it? 'Ow would half-a-dozen sparrows suit, then? Ha, ha. Don't you know there's a war on?"

Usually everyone rallied round together to solve this sort of problem, but for some reason this one was treated by the family as a test of individual enterprise. My uncles became secretive, given to whispering to flash spivs in pubs. My mother kept going off on long bus rides into the country.

Grannie even stooped to blackmailing Billy the milkman, knowing he kept a none-too-legal pig or two and some chickens at home. Didn't she keep back the kitchen waste to feed his porkers?

"....I'm only saying you ought to look after those who look after you, Billy," she told him as he sipped his tea in the kitchen. "There are people you don't want to get on the wrong side of, you know."

"Don't come down on me, Allie," he pleaded, breaking into a sweat that had nothing to do with the scalding tea. "I don't know where to turn for a bird meself. I can get you a nice leg o' pork."

Gran gave him a look that said if the boy hadn't been listening she'd tell him where he could shove his leg of pork. A bird, a big bird, it had to be.

On Christmas Eve I was in the kitchen peeling apples for Grannie when Uncle Alf hurried in with a large parcel wrapped in newspaper under his arm.

"Quick, Ma, shove this out of sight in the pantry," he said. "It's a turkey. Keep it under your hat."

At four my mother came home early, looking very mysterious, and produced a pair of ducks she claimed she'd won in a raffle. Later Uncle Bill arrived, grinning foolishly and hiccuping, and unwrapped newspaper from a large tin, dented where he'd dropped it outside the Royal Arms.

"S'American," he told us. "Tin o' turkey. All got t'do is warm 'er up (hic). Good ol' Yanks."

All that meat — and it wasn't over yet. We were still having breakfast on Christmas Day when Grandpa, who had been kept in the dark, came staggering up the path, his arms wrapped round a turkey almost as big as him.

He couldn't understand why he wasn't the hero of the hour.

\*\*\*\*\*\*\*\*\*\*

My social life took a step up when I moved to Peel Road. The boys there included Roger and the twins, Tim and Mark. Roger's father was a chief petty officer in the Royal Navy, and his mother was a studious, well-read woman who encouraged Roger and his elder brother George to read 'improving' books. She was determined to do the best for her boys. The twins were the younger sons of a schoolmaster. He and his wife were musicians and Roger and I were quite often invited to join the family for a musical session round the piano. Their mother played the piano and the father often accompanied us on the violin. The twins often performed solo; and very sweet-voiced they were. I recall taking real pleasure in Mark unselfconsciously and happily singing Barbara Allen and other English folk songs.

Grannie was delighted to find I had come under such civilizing influences, not least when the twins' mother came to the house to invite me to tea and deeply impressed Grannie with her social graces. She reported to me later: "Tim and Mark's mum complimented you on your good manners. Well done, just make sure you keep it up. Manners will take you a long way."

I did indeed learn a great deal by copying the example set by the twins, and I noticed that Roger did the same thing. We both started sounding our aitches and instead of saying "I'm going in for me tea" we carefully copied their "I'm going in for m' tea." A neat way of getting round the self-conscious trap of calling it 'my tea' — that would be going too far. The singing, too, certainly helped our diction.

Through the twins, Roger and I came into closer contact with the Vicar of Christ Church, the Reverend Sedgwick, he of the deep, carefully modulated voice heavy with the solemnity of the requiem mass. We knew him from his occasional, condescending appearances at Sunday School or from his more frequent visits to Newtown, a Church of England school.

The vicar was a regular visitor to the twins' house in Peel Road — which eventually led to Roger's downfall.

There was always an air of the devil about Roger, a rebellious spirit only just held in check. They were a typical older-younger brother pair, always bickering, often fighting. George was bigger and stronger, though Roger found ways to hit back in self-defence. I think most of us kids sensed that their mother favoured the younger son (as mothers tend to do) and that underlay the rivalry between them.

Roger was always more inclined to be the daredevil on our trips with the twins out into the country — George, of course, had his own chums. These forays were the idea of their father and Roger's mother, to introduce us to Nature. Nature was very much The Thing then. We were encouraged to go out into the wildgrounds, between Gosport and Lee-on-the-Solent, and the back country between Browndown, the shingly heathland fronting the sea, and inland, the old manor of Rowner, the estates of the Prideux-Brune family.

Off we would go, four of us carrying a packed lunch, notebook and pencil in our satchels. A penny bus ride along the Fareham road took us to Rowner Lane, and from there we would amble off into a vast empty space with no end to it. Present-day mums would have a fit. Here we were, eight-year-olds wandering around the perimeter of an operational airfield, RAF Grange, across farmland, through woods, in the middle of nowhere, in the middle of a war. I don't suppose any of us have ever been happier.

We climbed trees, finding an ancient oak that was hollow in the middle, and which we could scale from the inside. It was next to the church of St Mary the Virgin, which was old enough to have a Norman arched entrance and delightfully set among the trees, with a thatched cottage next door. We spent hours peering through the fence at the airmen and their wonderful planes — once we found the wreck of a crashed fighter dumped alongside the fence. Mark claimed it was a Barracuda.

Mostly though, we turned away from the airfield and into the golf links, always careful to go to ground whenever we saw any players. In the woods we built dens, collected acorns, conkers and interesting insects, and we crossed cornfields, collecting the ripened ears, rubbing them in our hands blowing away the chaff and chewing the kernels.

Amazingly we only got lost once, when we took the wrong lane and blundered along for what seemed like hours until we came to the church in the centre of Stubbington village. From there we found we needed a halfpenny extra all round to get the bus home. Bold Roger hit upon the idea of knocking on the vicar's door to borrow 2d. The old boy coughed up gruffly and sent his housekeeper out to make sure we got the right bus. We got it in the neck for being late for tea. But no-one ever thought of stopping us from going.

But it was also Roger who got us into trouble with our own vicar. It was the twins', birthday and we were at their house for tea — there was ice-cream, a rare treat in wartime. Both parents and the vicar, of course, joined in the games afterwards. Somehow the Reverend Sedgwick managed to bring an air of solemnity even into 'Pin the tail on the donkey', one of our party favourites, which when you come to think of it was no mean feat. Roger soon fixed all that.

There was a pause in the flow of the game and the twins' mother said: "Whose go is it next?" We were all jumping about with excitement and Roger hollered "It's old Sedgie's turn...."

The vicar was anything but amused. The parents were appalled. The temperature sank to freezing. No-one made any move to save it and the party expired. And it was a long time before Roger was invited to tea again.

He was also the victim of another incident around that time. In the nineteenth century the local bigwig had been Admiral Field, who lived in a grand house surrounded by an extensive estate. By World War II much of that had been developed for housing and only the big house remained, mostly boarded up and derelict, sitting in an acre or so of neglected garden between Grove Avenue and Carlton Road. Naturally we kids decided this near-ruin was haunted and got a great thrill out of being scared to go near it at twilight. The air of mystery was compounded by the long shadows thrown by a half-dozen ancient yew trees surrounding the place.

Under one of these beautiful but grim yews overhanging Carlton Road some builders had left a big pile of sand piled up against the fence. This was the scene of the drama.

It made a perfect sandpit for kids deprived of access to the beach at Stokes Bay, so Roger and I and other kids were quick to move in with buckets and spades. I remember on the day it happened I was absorbed in building fortifications, a row of sandcastles, while Roger and a couple of others were digging tunnels. The first I knew of any trouble was a sudden scream — I turned to see Roger sobbing and holding his head, blood pouring through his fingers. Apparently someone had hit him with the edge of a metal spade.

I clearly recall Roger being led away home by the other boys, terrified and still sobbing as I trailed along behind. As I crossed Peel Road to our gate, they were hurrying off down the other side and I heard a boy saying to Roger: "Say John Bull did it — say John Bull did it," over and over again.

Quite what I thought about that at the time, I don't recall. I went indoors and told Grannie what had happened, and as far as I was concerned that was it.

I started this recollection by calling Roger the victim — and he obviously was the subject of a vicious, if unthinking, attack. But he recovered quickly enough and seemed not to suffer any long-term damage. However, suddenly I turned out to be a victim, too. Innocent though I was, the story that I had 'done it' went round the neighbourhood. Invitations for John 'to come and play' or come to tea, or join a party, dried up. Especially hurtful was the fact that I was never asked to visit the twins' house again.

After the drama, Mum told me Roger's mother had come to the house and confronted Grannie, complaining that I had made this murderous attack on her younger boy, and adding the dramatic line: "He'll carry that mark to his grave." Grannie told her she sympathised and invited her to sit down and have a cup of tea — but that I had told her what happened and she was quite happy that I had certainly not hit Roger with a spade, or anything else. Incidentally my spade was made of wood. And there it was left.

Of course I knew the boys had lied, but I never talked about it. I think I assumed that in their shoes I'd have done the same thing. Roger and I never played together again; his mother had forbidden him from playing with me. And though we were in the same class at Newtown boys' school we simply kept clear of each other.

The incident meant that, in order to find new playmates, I fell back on the street arabs from Queen's Road. By climbing over the back wall of our house I was on the common ground of the two huge bombed sites that by now made up the greater part of Avenue Road. It wasn't long before this wasteland became our happy hunting ground. There we built dens, cooked spuds and a sort of vegetable stew, over open fires. It was the start of new adventures for me as I made the transition from genteel student of the natural world to a far more fascinating life as one of the Bomb Alley Kids.

\*\*\*\*\*\*\*\*\*\*

There was a sequel to the spade story some 20 years later. On a rare visit to Gosport, I bumped into Roger and George's mother in the High Street post office. We chatted for a while and she finally said: "Of course Roger will carry that scar you gave him to his grave." "Ah," I replied, "that may be....but you see I didn't hit him with the spade, or anything else."

"If you didn't hit him, who did?" She was peering intently into my face.

"I can't tell you," I said. "But I know the boys lied about it."

"Why would they do that?" I shook my head — but I had the clear impression that she knew, or thought she knew, the answer. She simply shook my hand and walked away.

The family pictured around the time of World War I: Auntie Gert,
Grandpa Alfred Ferré, Uncle Bill, and (front) Grannie with Edie,
who died as a child, and my mother Nell

# Chapter Eight
## Bomb Alley Kids

The wall at the end of our garden in Peel Road had been topped with broken glass set in cement to deter burglars, but my uncles had knocked out or ground down the shards of this mantrap — not in a sudden onrush of humanity, but so they could clamber over and take a short cut across the bomb-sites direct to their Sunday lunchtime pub, The Albert in Queen's Road.

Lacking mates to play with, I arranged a couple of soap-boxes so that I could see over the wall to watch the local kids. One day I heard shouts and yells from the bomb site....and rushed to my observation post.

A group of children were lined up in front of their den just over the wall from me, and most of the shouts were coming from the 'bommie' on the other side of the road, where a bigger gang were on the attack, lobbing stones and chunks of brick as they crept forward.

Though they were also hurling rubble at the attackers the set in front of me were smaller and younger and were being outflanked and forced back into their den. One boy turned and ran away, blood dripping from a cut on his head. Another spotted me and hollered: "Oy, Bully come and 'elp us, mate. They're gonna smash up our den."

I suppose I was just lonely enough to risk it, so I dropped over the wall and ran at a crouch up the alley and into the bushes that defined the den. I picked up a couple of bits of rubble and hurled them at the attackers. A tall boy called Jimmy grabbed my arm.

"Come with me," he ordered. "We'll try to get in behind them."

Jimmy was a born tactician (wartime kids do study such things). As our side fell back onto their den, the wings of the attackers tended to close into the middle. It meant Jimmy and me were able to pour in a fusillade of flanking fire and make a few lucky hits that stopped the advance. Trouble was, our success brought us to the attention of their commander, who promptly sent three of his wingmen charging our way.

"Fall back quick," said Jimmy, and we rushed back to join his friends in their camp. Inevitably, the enemy made a final rush and poured in, pushing us back into the alley against my garden wall. We dropped our stones and stuck our hands up — beaten and shamed.

"Whose damp?" said one of the newcomers — and I recognised him as one of the feared family of three brothers, all with speech impediments, who lived nearby.

"It's our camp now, aint it?" said his leader, a tall kid called John who shoved him out of the way just to show he was in charge. His pals were picking over the losers' weapons — fence posts and the like — and shields (dustbin lids, mostly rusty, and cooking pots). It wasn't much of a collection. In fact as dens go, even I could see it was pretty pathetic. Big John decided it wasn't worth the bother of smashing up.

"We're the Queen's Road Gang," he stated, "this is now our territory, same as the other bommies round here. Anybody want to join our gang?"

I stuck my hand up — and that's how I became a Bomb Alley Kid.

I first saw the name in the Daily Mirror. Our gang was probably typical. The thing was, we were totally unsupervised. Most fathers were servicemen away from home. Local bobbies and wardens generally had better things to do than chase unruly kids. So we got away with almost anything short of looting or murder. Newspapers of the day bewailed a reported 80 percent increase in juvenile crime.

Under the threat of invasion, the military had sealed off the seashore early in the war. Gosport kids, however, were left with the creeks, the Wildlands and — best of all, because they were on the doorstep so to speak — we now had the bomb sites. That's where the Bomb Alley Kids set up camp, built dens, and defended their territory against all-comers. Nowadays it would be graffiti-ed up with 'Bomb Alley Kids Rule, OK,' or maybe just our 'tags'.

The pecking order was led by Big John, bigger and taller than the rest and who preferred to be called Jono, then came Dave and Les then, a year younger, Bridges and me, known as Bully. When he was old enough we were also joined by Jono's younger brother George, and we sometimes (reluctantly) included Chris and Bobby, two runny-nosed nippers who were dumped on us to look after by their mothers.

As Jono put it: "Too tired to look after their own kids — lazy, idle cows."

We ruled an area roughly equivalent to the parish of Christchurch with occasional forays into the town, but always ready to clear out if we met the Townies. Similarly we rarely went to the Forton or Leesland areas....and definitely never to the northern shores of the Harbour, ruled by the scary Hardway Kingers (named after their famous local crabs, now sadly extinct).

As well as the extensive bombed sites in Queen's Road and Avenue Road, we had the moats which surrounded the old town, the ramparts, Haslar Creek, Alver Creek and our own private bit of muddy foreshore in the hidden Gasworks Creek which was tucked away between the gasworks proper and Walpole Park. There was a gas company footbridge across the mouth of this inlet, which incidentally was all mud at low tide, but we had our own secret access from Jamaica Place.

The seashore at Stokes Bay and Gilkicker were barred to us for the duration of the war, but we did have the canoe lake and the cockle pond in Walpole Park to swim in, or better still the municipal baths also in Walpole Park, if we had 3d to get in.

This kids' paradise was fed by the water of the moat, in turn fed by the sea. It was a Thirties sporting dream in municipal Art Deco, with spacious terraces and patios, a spectacular waterfall, a long, wide pool of clear water from three to seven feet deep, with a Mediterranean blue-painted bottom, and sunken inside the terraces as a protection against the (permanent) breeze.

At the eastern end, it had a water chute and a set of diving boards, which seemed to soar into the blue sky, and which was often the scene of some fancy gymnastics from the more athletic swimmers. It was a wonderful place on a warm August day — and I have always thought of it as a Gosport version of the Berlin Olympics films of Leni Riefenstahl.

Of course, like Lee Tower and the Penny Palace, it has long since been destroyed by the perennially unlucky borough council. But it lives on in townspeople's memories as 'the best thing Gosport ever did.'

We loved to duck under the waterfall and pretend we were in a jungle movie with the ex-swimming champ turned film star Johnny Weismuller. If we hadn't got 3d for a ticket we used to climb over the sluice gates in the moat just outside the pool's fence and, with a smart bit of acrobatics, grab the top of the fence and roll over to drop neatly onto the grass on the other side, one at a time. Three or four of us could make it before the attendants noticed....mostly they turned a blind eye.

Sometimes they'd grab you and march you back to the entrance and shove you out, threatening to ban you 'if we catch you again'....both sides understanding that the crime was not to get in, but to get caught getting in. The baths superintendent in those far-off days, just happened to be a cousin of one of our gang.

Someone once pointed out that there is no security system on earth that can keep out a gang of boys. Well, I can vouch for the fact. Our part of town was full of empty houses that people had locked up for the duration and evacuated themselves to 'safer' places out in the country. Generally we took that as an excuse to treat the place like our own. In most of these 'sealed' houses in the Stoke Road area I treated myself to a conducted tour, though I never took anything away with me.

For instance we were fairly intimate with Admiral Field's grand house in Grove Avenue, now deserted and boarded up. Once the gang went there late on a winter afternoon and toured the bedrooms, very daring, because, as everybody knew, the place was haunted. We moved about speaking in whispers, keeping very close to each other.

"Look," shouted Bridges suddenly, pointing at the window. We looked, I saw the crescent moon shining spookily through the branches of the nearest yew tree....we didn't wait for the wind to moan or the owl to hoot, we crashed down the stairs, struggling, pushing and shoving each other out of the kitchen door, and didn't stop running till we got to our den on the bommie.

We loved stealing fruit. Along the stretch of the disused railway line to Stokes Bay, sometimes still used for shunting, the railwaymen had little allotments. They (unknowingly) shared their strawberries, raspberries and gooseberries with us but, strangely, we never stole any of their veg.

We loved to raid the garden at Holy Trinity Vicarage, home of the awesome Canon Cyril Barclay, set alongside the high ramparts opposite his church. We used to take tin trays to the ramparts and slide down the grassy banks, turning at the last moment to avoid plunging straight into the moat. As the summer came on, the pears in the great, tall trees in the canon's garden were pure temptation on a hot day. We'd lie in the grass peering down the bank into the garden. The younger, nippier boys, Bridges and me usually, were sent in first as being harder for a well-fed parson to catch, and because he was thought more likely to go easy with us. Some hopes. I swear I can still feel the sting of the cane he swiped across my arse with his well-aimed, well-practised swing.

We used the same tactic at Bourton House, the mansion set between Elmhurst Road and Queen's Road, then a wartime Toc H social club for servicemen. A boy in my class, Andy, was the son of the manager, and I used to go and play with him. The garden was surrounded by trees and in one corner were some succulent apples and ripe plums. Of course, I was sent in first. I filled my shirt with apples and was climbing down the tree when a snarling great dog came bounding up. I swear I could feel his hot breath on my back as I hauled myself up to the highest fork I could reach. The animal was barking his head off and trying to shake the tree to get me down.

That's when Andy's father found me. "Come on down," he instructed, putting a choke chain on Fido, "Oh, it's John, isn't it?"

Grannie was mortified when he marched me home, and handed me over....red-faced with shame.

More successfully we made a raft — we were always making rafts or trying to plug the leaks in ancient and abandoned old boats and floating them about on Gasworks Creek. We had to be careful to keep out of the way of the gasmen who, with typical adult arrogance, considered it belonged to them. It was a free country wasn't it? One raft we made from three slender tree trunks lashed together was good enough to pole right across at high water to land on the shore just alongside an orchard at the bottom of a garden in Woodstock Road. The owner, who clearly thought he didn't need a fence along the creek, must have been really puzzled where his fruit was going.

Ever hear of the Mudlarks? They were kids who used to wade into the mud at Portsmouth Hard and beg for money from passers-by along the pier to the harbour station.

We once famously ventured over the water to Pompey as a gang to try it, lured by stories of how much money they made. Had we not all seen them when visiting Pompey with our families? They were always there at low tide as hundreds of people passed to and from the ferry or the station. The mudlarks would call out to them:

"Throw us a penny, Guv. Don't be mean....chuck it down, then."

We couldn't believe it....but even strong-minded people like my Grannie might throw a coin down into the mud. Then, quick as light, a near-naked, muddy urchin, boy or girl, would dive into the ooze, scoop up a handful, rub it between their hands and hold the penny up to show the crowd.

When there were young matelots about with their girlfriends, the trick was to shout:

"Oy, meanie, show us some silver," to shame them into throwing a Joey (3d) or a tanner (6d).

Matelots were paid fortnightly, so the mudlarks would also shout: "No snow, blank week?" in an attempt to challenge them to show off a bit. On the same principle, Dave said to the rest of us: "I'm sick of talking about it. Are we gonna have a go at it or not?"

So, scared though we were, we couldn't back down. However, we did recruit a couple of heavies, Fatty and his mate Robbo, on the promise of a share in the loot, and took the ferry across the harbour.

The drill was that from Portsmouth Hard you walked out along the public slipway well into the mudflats, changed into your swimming trunks leaving your clothes on the hard with your towel draped over them, then waded out into the mud getting as close as possible under the pier.

What about the opposition? Well, no doubt there were a few Pompey kids already at work, but a word or two from Fatty and his mate convinced them that it would be better to clear off for an early tea.

That was a mistake, as it happened. In the first place none of us had any experience of barking up the crowds to get them to throw money. We simply stood aimlessly, helplessly looking up as hundreds of potential customers hurried by on their way to the shops.

I had already lost my footing a couple of times in the mire and was covered in a filthy black slime. I had even managed to get some on my head and, as I stood miserably shivering in mud up to my bum, I could feel it drying into my hair....this was not how it was supposed to be. Fatty and his mate were getting restless, too. And they were apt to take out any disappointment on the nearest smaller kid. We were saved by the arrival of a group of real Pompey mudlarks who, after surveying us carefully from the slipway, decided to go for it anyway. In no time they were catcalling to the sailors and the manna from heaven started to trickle down.

One of them shouted up : "Chuck it flat, mate....keep it flat," meaning the coin needed to land flat on the mud to make it easy to find. A coin landing on edge might sink too quick for a kid to grab.

A 'splat' sounded near me and Dave, quick to react, surged towards the spot before the penny sank.

"S'mine," yelled a mudlark, pushing me in the back. But Dave dived in and grabbed the coin, rubbed the mud off and held it up to the crowd, and got a cheer for his efforts. More money started to fall. The crowd were quick to see we were ready to fight over it and started yelling us on. I soon discovered that there were more farthings and ha'pennies in their pockets than pennies or tanners, but cash was cash after all. The sight of about a dozen kids all covered in mud — the Pompey lads had blacked up their faces with it — having a glorious battle on the shore was worth chucking down a couple of pennies for.

Of course, we greenhorns had forgotten that we had nowhere to put our money. The real mudlarks had come with cocoa tins to stash their winnings. Once we had two coins we needed to find somewhere to put them, or we had no hands free to collect more. Never mind; the Pompey boys said we could use their tins and we'd divide up the money later. There were more of us, they pointed out, with a meaningful glance at Fatty and Robbo.

Jono and Dave agreed and we handed over our winnings. If anything, now we were on the same side, the 'battle' of the mudflats seemed to get tougher....we knew how to put on a good show all right. By the time the tide started to seep back in I'd handed out a few thumps and collected a few bruises, too. Still, it would be worth it, wouldn't it? We were in happy mood as we washed the mud off in the incoming sea, dried off with our towels, washed the mud off the money, and got dressed. At this point, a pair of older youths came sauntering down the slipway, sharing a fag.

"Wotcher, boys" one said to the mudlarks, "see you got a bit of 'elp today, 'en. 'Ow much yer got?" And he picked up the cocoa tins...."Oh, not bad," he said, "there could be a coupla quid 'ere."

We looked at each other baffled. One of our Pompey friends explained: "That's my brother and his mate....we might be lucky and get a cup of tea out of it. You lot best get off 'ome." Fatty and his mate weighed up the opposition briefly....before joining the rest of us as we trailed off back to Gosport.

\*\*\*\*\*\*\*\*\*\*

With all these creeks around, we had plenty of places to go fishing. But we soon discovered that sitting on the end of a line waiting for a bite was more boring than going to school.

Dave suggested we try spearing fish, like we'd seen loin-clothed natives do in films. In those days the creeks were teeming with plaice, dabs, flounders and so on, all known to us as flatties. Indeed in the hungry Thirties there were out-of-work men who specialised in 'groping' for them, catching them practically with their bare hands — something to feed the kids.

"Spear them with what?" Jono asked, always ready to put the mockers on any idea that didn't come from him.

"Remember when we pulled out the railings and sharpened up the ends?" Dave reminded him. "We could do that again."

I seem to remember that in our den we had four or five of these 'railings' — iron rods that had been forced out of their concrete bases and had their points sharpened up with a steel file borrowed from somebody's toolbox. We carted them over to Alver Creek, took off our plimmies, rolled up the legs of our shorts and waded out into the shallow water.

"Try not to stir up the mud or you won't see the fish," Jono instructed, placing himself back in charge.

Despite the silt we kicked up the water was clear enough to see anything that moved, and soon we spotted a flattie. Instantly we all hurled our spears at it. A hefty collection of ironmongery clattered onto the creek bed.

"This won't do, boys," said Dave. "One at a time's best."

"I'll go first," said Jono, reminding him who was top kick.

I forget who it was, but one of us actually did spear a respectable plaice. We made a big thing of marching up Queen's Road holding up the railing with the fish impaled on it. Then we cooked it over a fire on the bommie and passed it round so that everyone had a taste, along with a pen'orth of chips each from the chippy in Queen's Road. Thus we tasted the bliss of independence.

We did in fact get our hands on some real spears later. The details are vague (because their acquisition from a 'sealed up' house in Peel Road was a deep secret). These spears were identical to the ones we'd seen in a church film show that depicted a mutiny of native 'converts' in Africa and the massacre of the missionaries.

To us they were quite wonderful, about five feet long with shafts of ebony and broad blades, sharp as razors. They balanced beautifully in the hand and there was no doubt that this was the real thing. We took them to Admiral Field's overgrown garden to try them out.

"Watch this," said Les launching his spear at a tree. It flew straight and with a satisfying 'thunk' embedded itself deep in the trunk.

Then Dave threw the other one — while the rest of us stood entranced.

"Can I have a go, please?" It wasn't like Jono to be humble. Clearly the spears were something outstanding.

"You'll have to get everybody to swear an oath not to tell about this, doncha think?" said Dave, ever the diplomat. Jono agreed and lined us all up with our hands touching the shaft of a spear.

"Repeat after me," he said solemnly. " I swear on the grave of my mother (here there was a sharp intake of breath all round — this was really serious) that I will never tell about the sp...." Dave held up a hand to interrupt.

"Better not say what," he said. Jono nodded and started again with us all repeating the oath.

"....I swear on the grave of my mother I will never tell about the secret things. Cross me 'eart and hope to die."

Eventually, of course, a bobby called at Jono's house and took the wonderful spears away. There was talk of the juvenile court, but I don't think anything came of it.

There was a similar outcome the time we had the musket. I have no idea where that came from. It just appeared one day in the den. A little bit rusty along the barrel. It obviously pre-dated the rifle, probably muzzle-loading, and the firing mechanism was missing — it was no more than a tube really, with a polished walnut stock and a trigger guard, but no trigger.

It was knocking about the den for quite a while. We proudly marched about with it — until it was seen by a couple of older boys who seemed quite interested in it.

"Where did you get the blunderbus?" they asked. "Why don't you try firing it?"

It turned out that they offered to supply the gunpowder, or some kind of charge anyway, if we got some ammunition.

"Where are we going to get ammo?" said Jono.

"Have you got any marbles? This looks about the right size to fire them."

We were definitely onto something here. The boys turned out to be sea cadets — with know-how and access to various interesting things. A few days later they showed up with a few simple 'charges,' some slowmatch and a handful of marbles, and took over Bess the Blunderbuss. To be on the safe side we carried it all down to Gasworks Creek.

They stuck Bess's stock firmly in the earth, leaning the barrel over a couple of sandbags and pointing into the air. They then lit the fuse and ran back to crouch down with us. Bess fizzed away for a while, then with a sharp crack the wad and marble flew up into the air to splash down into the mud about 50 feet away. The gang were very impressed.

Unfortunately the shot also captured the attention of the nosy blokes at the gasworks....and sure enough a few days later a copper showed up at Jono's home and took Bess away.

"Prob'ly gonna give 'er to the 'ome Guard," said Les.

(In the enlightened twenty-first century, of course, the Armed Response Unit would rush to the scene and spray enough lead to wipe out the Queen's Road Gang. With wonderful English logic the government arms the police — always a dangerous mistake — who then warn kids that playing with toy guns can get them shot.)

Now and again we would 'find' some lead, just lying around 'unattended' and we would give it a safe home in our den. A week or two later we would load up our soap-box cart with whatever scrap metal we had been able to collect and wheel it down to the scrap merchant. We called him the Tin Man, a discreet old bloke who rarely asked too many questions. I used to love poking about among the amazing piles of stuff cluttering up his yard down by Clarence Square.

"What's this then, mister?"

"They're snake skins, put 'em down."

"Where'd they come from then?"

"People catch the snakes and skin 'em, and I  buy 'em off of them."

We looked at each other — we knew where there were plenty of snakes, didn't we?

And so, after he'd given us a short lesson in skinning and drying, we made plans for an excursion to the Wildlands on Saturday.

Jono and Dave made us all wear wellies and gloves to avoid being bitten. I was terrified of snakes and said so.

"Only the adders are poisonous," Jono said. "They're the ones with the V for Viper on their necks — or where their necks would be if they 'ad 'em. The slow-worms and the grass snakes can't hurt you. You stick to them and you'll be all right."

And that is how I found myself sitting alongside a smoky fire, somewhere in the spacious undergrowth of the Wildlands at Browndown, alongside the muddy stream of the Alver, Gosport's only river....and more like a reed-filled drainage ditch.

God knows where it started from, as far as we were concerned it began at Apple Dumpling Bridge, a Wildlands landmark, and it ran across the marsh and shingle through the gorse to meet the sea via a concrete culvert at the western end of Stokes Bay.

Not that there was that much river to see. For long sections in the summer, the water was completely hidden by the lush reedbeds growing on either side. Lovely for the ducks and all other kinds of avian life, a twitcher's paradise no doubt, but to lads used to playing with rafts, leaky boats and a home-made canoe, a navigational dead loss.

The day was stifling. I'd discarded my gloves and spent most of the time lying on my back in the grass, staring at the pale green treetops. It was like the jungle in here. I only too easily pictured a Japanese soldier creeping soundlessly through the bamboo. In the comics these caricature Nips (hideously ugly and all wearing glasses) were famous for being the sneakiest jungle fighters in the world, totally invisible until they opened fire, or stuck a bayonet in your guts.

The hum of insects and the twittering of birds was noisy to say the least. I swear I heard monkeys chattering in the treetops.

Jono had ordered me to stay and guard the camp and to keep an eye on the half-dozen dead snakes drying over the fire, hung on the wire we had arranged as a spit. The older boys were pretty good at trapping a snake by jabbing a forked stick over its neck and pushing down hard, then clubbing it to death with one heavy blow.

"Try to do it first time," the Tin Man had warned us. "I don't want the heads, but I don't want the skin damaged too much." I nearly threw up every time I thought about it.

As predicted I was utterly hopeless at catching the slimy things — the others seemed to be able to spot them wriggling through the grass, but to me they were invisible. So I was the campfire man. The snakes seemed to be drying nicely, I ran a cautious finger down the biggest, an adder with a sinister pattern of V markings down its back. It didn't feel moist at all.

Suddenly the snake gave a sharp hiss and struck at my hand. It was still alive! It bit me!

I roll away from the fire and scream blue murder — shouting and hollering: "Jono....Dave....help me. Help quick help me. Help....help!"

I am sure I am going to die. In seconds. I can feel a numbness creeping up my arm. Paralysis....setting in already! Oh, my God. I shout louder.

"Wassup? Stop screaming, you fool," Dave charges out of the jungle and grabs hold of me. Jono is right behind him. Both of them crouch over me.

"Wassup wiv him?"

"Snake....bit me," I sob. "I'm dying...."

"Shut up. Course yer not gonna die," Jono says, giving me a good shake. "Where d'e bite yer?" I hold up my hand.

"That it?" Dave points to a red mark on my wrist. "Stop crying, you baby. Show me."

Jono grabs my wrist, picks up the razor blade we use for skinning snakes and nicks the skin. Then he bends over and sucks my wrist. He gobs a mouthful of blood on the ground. Then repeats the treatment twice.

"Lie down and keep real still," he tells me. "I don't think you've been bit, but keep still and the poison won't spread. And keep quiet. Be brave."

I lie back on the grass and make a big effort to stop snivelling. Dave pulls a grubby hankie from his pocket and winds it round my wrist, tying the ends tightly together. The other two kids have arrived by now and they stand solemn-eyed gazing down at me.

Bridges finally says: "Ee's probly gonna be orlright. Ed'd be 'avin' the fits by now if an adder got 'im."

Everyone (except me) seemed satisfied with this diagnosis. Dave carefully prodded the snake I thought still alive, pronounced it really, really dead — and they got on with the skinning. As I recall, Tin Man gave us half-a-crown (12 1/2p) for the lot.

Diving for cash....mudlarks at work under Portsmouth Harbour station

[Picture: 'The News,' Portsmouth]

# Chapter Nine
## Alley-Alley Allover

For some reason no-one has ever explained, when I was at junior school which we were supposed to leave at 11, we had boys right up to 14. This was Newtown Boys' School, also known as Joseph Street School because it lay halfway down that street which ran between Stoke Road and the gasworks. Opposite was a burned out blacksmith's forge, a big attraction for us kids, but resulting in a sharp caning if you were caught inside.

While the infant school could lay claim to early twentieth century style, a sort of Towards Art Nouveau, Joseph Street was a Victorian relic with stunted mock Norman arched lobbies and tall classrooms with huge windows and stoves that burned coke brought up from the gasworks. We used to make up our own ink from powder mixed with water, and the pens were just little metal nibs with a sort of cuff that we fitted over the end of a piece of raw wood, no more than a twig really.

We had four teachers: headmaster Alfred Germain ('Old German' to us, naturally); Mr Mitchell, who was 100 years old and only about four feet tall; Mr Frampton, a bit of a dandy in his leather driving gloves, and who from time to time turned yellow, due to some illness that we kids all assumed was 'yellow jaundice'; and Mr Budge, with a cruel twist to his mouth like Captain Bligh of the Bounty, as played by Charles Laughton. All the boys respected Old German, disbelieved everything Mr Mitchell said, loved Mr Frampton and hated Old Budgie.

During the daylight air raids on Portsmouth and Gosport, lessons were stopped and we were marched out to the two long, brick-built shelters in the playgound. We sat on benches and, I suppose to take our minds off the raid, the teachers encouraged boys to come out to the front and tell stories to the others. The headmaster often called me out because he knew I read a lot and could remember the stories. But the real star of these sessions was Bernie, a tough-looking boy, older than me, who had real talent for making up streetwise fairy tales.

"....so this funny little man, who was some kind of elf, he said to the two boys: 'You 'ave been so kind to me, 'elping me across the creek, carrying me over the mud, that I am going to give you a wish.'"

"You mean we can 'ave anyfink we like?" said Ted.

"Anyfink," said the funny little elf. "Just name it."

Then Bernie, who had a showman's sense of suspense, would say: "I'll tell you what the boys wished for next time we 'ave an air-raid." And it would be someone else's turn with a new tale.

As daylight raids gave way to night bombing, the shelters were hardly used in school hours — except by us kids at playtime and then only on sunny days. This was for playing 'Planes.' We discovered that by standing in the doorway of the shelter with a small mirror or even a piece of shiny metal, facing the sun, you could divert a long beam of sunlight into the darkness inside, just like a searchlight.

Boys would hold their arms out like wings and run about inside the shelter making aeroplane noises: roaring engines and chattering cannon fire. The din was colossal. Half-a-dozen searchlights criss-crossed the air, directed by the boys with mirrors, stationed in the doorways at each end. If they lit up your face, you were hit and grounded for the rest of playtime.

When the beam hit you in the eyes with searing brightness you felt as if you really had been shot and I remember the shock of it clearly. I'd reel away spinning, one arm bent to signify damage, and slump down to the ground.

Occasionally reality did burst in on our little world of war games. When HMS Hood went down leaving only three survivors, she also left a lot of young widows and orphaned children in Gosport because she was a Pompey-manned ship. It made women like my mother with a husband at sea, very quiet, very thoughtful.

My father served in a destroyer, HMS Kimberley — at Narvik, then in the Med, based on Alexandria, escorting convoys to Malta and supporting troops ashore. Other boys had fathers in the Army, in the Hampshire Regiment, serving in the Western Desert with the Eighth Army, the Desert Rats, or veterans of the retreat in France sweating it out in a prisoner of war camp, like three of our family's uncles.

And then there were the walking wounded among the kids, too. One boy, called Jenson, limped about the playground with a badly mangled leg, the flesh behind his knee all stitched up and knotted.

**********

Newtown Boys' School laid lasting foundations to my education. It was there that I found a love of stories. Old Mitchell used to ensure total silence in his class by reading to us what we called 'books about the olden days.' The stories, usually about robbers, such as highwaymen and pirates, were set in old inns, or castles; or were about Arabia, or the jungles of India, the snowy wastes of Russia, or even the wild west of America.

Maths, from Old Budgie, was less popular, although the swine used to specialise in fast mental arithmetic; he taught us many a short cut — and I can still amaze younger people today with my ability to multiply and divide in my head. Thanks, Budgie.

Some things I recall learning in the playground by rote, as instructed by older boys who had gone through the mill. However at about the same time as I was being prepared for Confirmation I was also learning the circulation of the blood for First Aid lessons — and even now, all these years later, sometimes find my semi-conscious mind tends to nonsense up phrases like:

'He became incarnate of the virgin Mary....through the lungs to be purified....' when reciting the Creed at Mass.

\*\*\*\*\*\*\*\*\*\*

One morning after another night raid, I got to school and found the playground empty. A teacher was on duty telling everybody to go straight in. Everyone was very quiet and there were a number of empty desks in my class. Mr Germain came in and told us that a bomb had fallen on a row of houses near South Street and some of our school friends were among the casualties. He told it simply and gently and then sent us home.

Rumour said that a huge 'landmine', the bomb everybody dreaded most of all, had hit the area. From

Walpole Park you could see that it had devastated a whole row of the old terrace houses in Church Path off South Street.

There was a heavy toll of casualties, but the official list of the dead mentions only one family — a young widow, Mary Reekie, and her children Michael John (11) and Pamela Mary (8).

I don't recall who was injured, but I know some of our school mates were taken to hospital. The horror of that attack was a nightmare that anyone who lived in Gosport will never forget. But at the time it was something of a nine-day wonder, because it happened on May 23 1944 and, within a fortnight on June 6, it was overshadowed by the allied armies pouring across the Channel and onto the beaches of Normandy.

\*\*\*\*\*\*\*\*\*\*

We used to have singing lessons, conducted by Mr Germain. He had big sheets of words that he used to hang over the blackboard. He'd sit at the piano, play the tune through, and translate it into tonic sol-fa for us, sometimes calling out a group of four lads to sing together.

We had Oh for the Wings of a Dove, Come into the Garden Maud, The Road to the Isles, and a few patriotic numbers like Hearts of Oak and Rule Britannia. Often we'd sing a roundsong, which we all liked. Old Macdonald had a Farm, with animal noises, was a great favourite. One day as we were roaring out Jerusalem, Mr Germain suddenly stopped playing. One by one our voices faltered and we finally fell silent.

He got up from the piano, walked across to the window and stood looking out over the playground. Then, he put his face in his hands. All the boys sat stock still. We could see the tears running down his cheeks. The headmaster was weeping.

It seemed to go on for a long time. Some of the boys had tears in their eyes. I had trouble with a lump in my throat. Then Mr Germain wiped his face with his hankie and took a deep breath:

"All together now...." He crashed out a series of chords on the old piano and at the top of his voice started singing — "Old Mac-donald had a Fa—aar-m—" and we all joined in, "Eee—eye—Eee—eye—OOOOh!"

\*\*\*\*\*\*\*\*\*\*

We boys used to wear short trousers and, since we lived in a town that looked upon the Royal Navy as a sort of milch cow, most of these were made from blue uniform serge. Somehow the material would disappear from official stores and re-appear in the homes of navy families. Imagine the effect of serge trousers rubbing on thighs already reddened sore by a raw wind on a freezing January day. How we yearned for long trousers. But you had to be at least 13, or a very tall 12 before they'd let you. It would have been a kindness for a boy like Jenson to wear long trousers to hide his scarred leg....but no-one seemed to have thought of that.

As with long trousers, footwear had similar rules. All us kids went into stout black leather boots at about five, the kind Rupert Bear still wears. They were built to withstand heavy use by boys apt to climb walls, and kick stones about. To make them last even longer, most fathers fitted blakeys to the soles, heavy metal studs that took a lot of wear.

We used to find a street with a smooth concrete surface, without tarmac — Avenue Road was ideal, and Joseph Street was good, too — and crouch down while two other boys each grabbed an arm and raced off pulling you over the ground. Great fun. And when you stopped you tried to push your studs against your pal's leg, the blakeys now being red-hot from the friction. We used to call it 'tattooing' because the image burnt into the leg lasted a couple of days.

The boots were tough....and so were the games we played. We had our own version of the Eton Wall Game at Newtown. And bear in mind that some of the kids were hefty lads up to the age of 14.

This was 'Alley-Alley Allover,' played in two teams of half-a dozen or so. It was started off by a big anchorman — often we used Fatty Prescott — who'd stand with his back against the high brick wall at the back of the playground. Then a boy would bend over with his arms round Fatty, presenting a back, as in leap-frog, and the other four or five in the team joined on one by one.

The enemy had to run, one by one, leapfrog onto the backs, and try to wriggle as far up the line as possible. As more and more piled on, the crouching team had to brace themselves to take the shock of heavy bodies landing on their backs. A collapse meant you'd lost. But the other team didn't win unless they all were in place long enough to shout 'Alley-Alley Allover.'

Fatty used to complain that he got his head banged against the wall. But he really was the only one capable of standing up to the impact of six flying bodies one after the other. If anyone had the hardest job it was the guy holding him by the waist — I know because often that would be me. And I did used to get my head banged against the wall if the whole gang collapsed like sacks of spuds.

Then there was British Bulldog. Everyone lined up on one side of the playground. One boy was chosen as a bulldog to stand alone in the middle. A shout of 'GO' and everyone charged across to the other side — the kid in the middle had to grab a boy and hold him until the others were across. This boy then joined the bulldog in the middle....and so on until everyone had been caught.

The more bulldogs in the middle, the tougher the game became — because in no time at all there were six or more and they were inclined to single one kid out of the rush and beat him to the ground. That's when you tended to get an elbow in your face, causing a nosebleed, a punch in the guts that doubled you over, a crafty kick or three....and finally some serious bruises when several heavy bodies trampled you into the ground.

Obviously it was best to pull out early in the game when only one or two bulldogs were in the middle, by allowing yourself to be held back. That way you could join in the punching and kicking. However, if you did that too often, the crowd would start calling 'scaredy, scaredy' and the bulldogs would let you through until there were enough of them to do you some damage.

Cruel game, eh?

At home one day Uncle Alf noticed my cut lip and I told him it was from British Bulldog.

"Hear that, Bill," he called to his brother, "they been playing British Bulldog."

"Yeah?" said Bill. "Well I'm blessed....things don't change much, do they?"

They both chuckled a bit....clearly in a mood of happy nostalgia. I frowned at Les, one of my mates who happened to be there at the time.

"I know," he said. "I expected a bit of sympathy from my big brother when I had that black eye. An' 'e laughed like a drain. Sadistic bastard."

There was another equally brutal game, Cavaliers and Roundheads. I don't know where they came into it, except that it involved people hurling a tennis ball at each other. I can't remember the rules, or how it worked, except you wound your hankie round your fist in order to punch the ball away when someone threw it at you. And I can recall that when that ball hit you, you got a good idea of what a musket ball in the back felt like.

# Chapter Ten
# Man Dressed as a Pongo

My poor old grandfather went increasingly downhill at Peel Road. He had been (just) too old for the Great War and in the hungry years afterwards played an unassuming role as the silent partner to my very capable grandmother. His greatest times, of which he was very proud, were when he had been the best-known bookie's runner in town.

He had some schooling and his family, the Ferrés, had been relatively comfortably off. I never really knew much about his background, any more than did my older cousins. However, he managed to bring up four children of his own, plus the two he and Grannie took in as teenagers when their parents drowned.

The story was that at some time he had come into a small family legacy. It was an understood thing that Grandpa's share brought him in a steady pound or so a week: enough, with his modest income from racing, for him to keep his head above water without worrying about a regular job. By the time I was born in 1935 he would have had little enough, God knows, but taken one thing with another his income covered his likely outgoings and allowed a few luxuries in the way of beer and baccy. And, besides, in 1939 he was able to pick up the basic old-age pension.

Now the legacy story could well have been a cover invented to stop officialdom wondering how he lived without a proper job, while he got on with the betting.

That might make sense. However, townspeople often said he "always had an air of independence about him."

I never knew him leave the house without wearing a suit, usually black or navy blue, a little crumpled maybe, but with a stiff collar and a quiet tie. Like most of the men his age, he always wore a waistcoat, complete with watch and chain. His feet were bad, from neglect and the wearing of cheap, ill-fitting boots as a young man. So he couldn't walk very far, or very fast. As the war went on he (and others like him) found himself increasingly sidelined. Everyone was so busy surviving they had no time to indulge 'passengers' and, harsh though that seems, most older people understood and tried to adapt to a sort of 'advisory role.'

Unlike his older brother William, Grandpa had no time for organisations like the Masons or the Buffs, preferring to spend his leisure time with his pals at The Albert. Earlier in the war he did, of course, become a fire watcher, and proudly wore his red and black armband.

"The Nazi colours," his brother William, said nastily. By the time the Blitz really got going it was agreed by the ARP that even that job was too much for Grandpa.

From my baby days he became a great pal of mine. He'd take me out in my pram or pushchair for a stroll along the front at Stokes Bay, and later there was our lawless conspiracy as we walked the town picking up the betting slips. Looking back I realise I loved him totally without reservation, not something I can say about even a few.

While playing with him once when I was about four, I deliberately stuck a silver pencil in his ear. It had a sharp point like a stiletto and the blood flowed. He forgave me instantly, I know, and we both burst into tears. We sat for a long time hugging each other afterwards.

I can still feel the pain of that stupid jab.

When I first was old enough to notice, he and Grannie would often have a falling out over the household management, or maybe his absence from the fold, and therefore the chores. They had some (to me) fascinating rows which never resolved anything, ending as they did in a fruitless slanging match:

Grandpa: Arseholes then....

Grannie: Ten a penny....

But as the risk of air-raids — even tip-and-run raids — lessened, Grandpa found walking increasingly tough on his feet. He found more excuses not to go far, or to avoid going out at all. On fine days he was happy just to sit in the garden. I also noticed that he and Grannie stopped bickering; she patiently nursed him and their relationship moved into a different dimension. Mum also became more anxious to please him, and the uncles were quick to make sure he had his share of baccy and old ale.

Grandpa still had an easy smile, but he was markedly less inclined to chat. Eventually the uncles cleared out the downstairs front room and moved his bed in. The doctor and the district nurse began to drop in more frequently and eventually I overheard Grannie whispering to our neighbour....

"It's dropsy — there's no hope really. It's just a matter of time."

Auntie Gert and her daughters began to look in more often. I recall one visit when she brought my cousin Winston (born 1940 of course) and I was told to play with him in the garden. I showed him my Tommy gun, rattling off a pretend spray of bullets. Winston instantly rushed over to me, holding a finger to his lips.

"Sh, sh....," he lisped, "Grandpa....be quiet."

I stopped shooting, Oh, the shame of it. Shown up by my infant cousin.

Grandpa had been a choirboy in his youth, and the undertaker dressed him for burial in a shirt with a frill and a lacy collar, which gave him a peaceful, almost angelic look. He was laid in his coffin in the best room, for everyone to pay their final respects. The family decided I was old enough to be included. I was very nervous about this and held on tight to Mum's hand as we stood by the coffin. She leaned over weeping to give her father a last kiss. Without prompting I laid my cheek against his cheek; it was a long time before the feel of his smooth, cold face against my face faded from my memory.

Grandpa is buried in Ann's Hill cemetery, not far from his older daughter, my Auntie Gert, uncle Jim and their son Jimmy, the last members of the family to be buried rather than cremated.

\*\*\*\*\*\*\*\*\*\*

His passing foreshadowed big changes for all of us. One day, probably a Saturday, I was playing marbles on the living room floor. My favourite real marble (as opposed to a cheap imitation glass alley), the all-white one with the pools of deep blue patterning the surface, escaped and rolled under the piano.

I grabbed the poker from the fire-iron stand, threw myself flat on the floor and reached under the piano with it to rescue Bluey before it was lost for ever....as things usually are when they roll under the piano. My awkward prone position put a big strain on my breathing, and I couldn't get a clear swipe at it. Finally, I made contact and heard the marble roll along the floor....gently does it....

"John!" My Grannie calling from the doorway.

"Yeah?" Not looking up, concentrating on the marble.

"Here's someone to see you. Get up!"

"Blast," I think. I lever myself up into a sitting position. Grannie is holding the door open and standing alongside is a sheepish looking bloke in pongo's uniform. Is it a uniform? The tunic is a much darker khaki than the trousers. Looks a mess.

"Come and meet your Dad, then," she says. "He's come home from the war!"

Did she say Dad? Is she making a joke? I look unhappily from face to face. They are both smiling. But how can this awkward, messed-up pongo be my wonderful tiddly-sailor father? Had the woman gone mad?

He shuffles forward and reaches out to touch me....but I leap out of range and stand behind the sofa.

Poor man. His smile slips to one side.

"Hey," says Grannie. "It's your Dad, home from the war. At least say 'Hello'. She turns to him: "Best sit down....let him get used to you. It's probably a bit of a shock....after all it's been years...." The words dry up. He looks down at her, arms hanging loosely at his sides.

"I'll leave you together for a bit," says Grannie, uncharacteristically missing the point. How could she leave me with this strange pongo? What's going on here?

I rush over and throw my arms around her. She sighs and waves him to a chair while we both flee to the kitchen, where for the rest of the morning I refuse to leave her side.

Not the best start, then. I've learned since that that was pretty typical of the first contact between kids and their long-gone dads. It was one of the effects that men and their children had suffered since wars began. The Greeks and the Romans knew about it — why didn't the British government? Maybe it was just another thing everyone forgot in that strange euphoria that comes when the bugles start to blow. I believe that, later, psycho-babblers were eloquent about 'returned hero trauma' at the end of the war.

However, that wasn't of much help to me or my Dad. For us it was a ferocious head-on shock. My mother had encouraged me to work on an idealised picture of my absent idol since 1939.

"Here's a picture of Daddy in his uniform. Doesn't he look smart?"

And among my treasured souvenirs is a hand-coloured photograph of HMS Kimberley, my father's destroyer, bravely steaming across the waves, on the Christmas card he sent in 1940.

"Daddy's ship has lots of guns....and he is the one who fires the torpedoes," Mum told me. As us bomb-alley kids would say, "Go on, Dad, sink the bastards."

And what have I got here....a sorry-looking refugee in creased khaki, looking like something the cat dragged in. No thanks.

It worked both ways, too.

Scapa Flow 1939:

"Who's this then, Johnny?" — "Oh, that's my wife, Nell."

"Cor, you lucky bugger — looks like one of them fill-um stars, Bette Davis, ain't it?"

I didn't see my father for three years — he sent me this
rare card in 1940

A happy day, a peaceful day.

May Easter bring in everyway,

And every heart with gladness thrill,

In memory of Peace and all goodwill.

*To my Darling & Baby John.*

*From Daddy* xxxxxxxxxx xx.

— *//* —

Somewhere in the Med 1941:

"Who's the cowboy, Johnny? Billy the Kid?"

"That's my boy. The cowboy outfit was his Christmas present, nearly two years ago. He's a bit bigger now. At the boys' school."

"Yeah? Nice lookin' lad — well done, Johnny."

For a moment my father feels taller, braver — forgetting how scared he was yesterday when the convoy was strafed and bombed by the Luftwaffe. Maybe he will see that day that they all long for, but fear they may never see, when 'it's all over' and the boys come home.

There'll be brass bands playing, smiling wives and girlfriends blowing kisses, the king handing out medals....and the children, well-dressed, smiling, waving their little union jacks....

And what did Johnny, my old man, get? A harrassed mother-in-law, turban round her head, flour-coated hands. His lovely wife working at the munitions yard....and this lumpy boy, what is he....nine....ten? A lippy street urchin, badly in need of some discipline. "Surely my boy isn't one of these Bomb Alley Kids we've heard about?"

Of course, later that first day I did recognise him when I heard him speak and looked more closely. And I noticed the Royal Navy flashes on the shoulders of his khaki battledress.

"Yes, I'm still in the navy," he told me gently, "I just haven't got a proper uniform right now. Lost all my stuff when the ship sank. I'll get one before I come and see you again. Promise." He stayed the night, but in the morning when I woke he was gone. For a while I thought I might have dreamt the whole thing.

Despite all he'd been through, the navy only gave him a few days compassionate leave because of his status as a 'wounded survivor'. His left wrist had been smashed during an air-raid, and he wound up with a scaphoid fracture that, despite years of hospital treatment, never did properly mend. He and Mum went off for a few days' holiday and then he was back in the Andrew, albeit on 'light' duties — interrupted by many a visit to the Royal Naval Hospital Haslar, handily located just over the creek from our house.

The next time I saw him he was in full square-rig with wide bell-bottomed trousers, a torso-hugging jumper topped off by a silk neckerchief, rolled just so, and a real old salt's collar, the colour washed out pale blue as an autumn sky. On his sleeve, three deep, red stripes, his long-service and Good Conduct badges. His round cap was decorated with a ribbon with a fancy bow (done I believe with a razor) and his black shoes shone like dancing pumps.

Further adjustments to our relationship were forthcoming. He brought with him a kitbag which he'd stored safe in barracks somewhere — in case of shipwreck. From it he produced some 60 complete sets of fag cards, lovingly collected, swapped and hoarded down the years. There were Stars of the Silver Screen, the Kings and Queens of England, Famous Racing Cars, The History of Flight, Great Railway Engines....as far as kids were concerned, a sailor home from sea couldn't have done better if he'd walked in with Cap'n Flint's Treasure and a parrot on his shoulder shouting "pieces of eight!"

The fag cards made me king of Mr Frampton's class at Newtown School. I was even proud to parade my old man in his sailor's rig up and down Gosport High Street. Most of my mates still had fathers away at sea.

Dad was back — but we didn't see much of him as he moved around from barracks to hospital and back as the medics tried to assess his chances of returning to active duty. They even called it a 'survey,' as if he'd been a ship.

I recall one day when I found him sitting on the arm of a chair in the drawing room, looking out at the garden. I was idly messing about, probably with my beloved fag cards, when I became aware that Dad was snuffling a bit. I looked up and saw the tears streaming down his face. We sat like that for a very long time....until I found the guts to crawl over to him and put my arms round his legs and my face against his knee. I don't know how long we stayed like that, but neither of us said a word about it. Not then, not later.

His experiences at sea remained a mystery to me.

I remember Mum explaining: "He just doesn't want to talk about it. His brothers, Bill and George, they were in the Great War, in the trenches, and those old soldiers had their own unwritten code — 'never talk about it to anyone who wasn't there.'

"They'll tell you all sorts of stories about their adventures in France, and they'll tell blokes in the pub tales of the 'mamselles' they kissed, but the trenches, no. They will sing those wonderful ditties they made up to music hall favourites and hymn tunes — but the mud, the blood and the whizz-bangs, forget it. That's sacred ground, see. And it's the same with your Dad. So don't ask, son."

In fact he would happily relate some strange thing that happened to him, often ruefully, or some story with a funny ending, what the matelots called 'spinning a dit.'

That's how I later came to piece together some of the fighting he saw while serving in the destroyer HMS Kimberley. We were at a museum in Southampton with my children one time when we came upon a model of the ship in a glass case. Not surprisingly, since she was built there at Thorneycroft's yard on the River Itchen.

Dad pointed out various features....the guns, the torpedo tubes....

"You see that little corner there, in front of the starboard tubes ? That was a favourite place of mine to get my head down," he told us. "Well, that was where I was with my oppo Dan, oh, let's see, that would have been in the summer of 1941....we were part of a force sent to soften up the Vichy (German controlled French forces) up in Syria or Lebanon...."

By now, quite a little crowd has gathered round us, taking an interest in this living history lesson.

"One of our destroyers, Janus, had taken several hits from enemy ships or shore batteries and we were ordered to take her under tow, into Haifa for repairs. Of course, it took time to fix the tow, and in the meantime we had to just lie there — sitting ducks under the enemy shore guns."

"It seemed to go on for ever. Me and Dan were lying on the deck, just there," he pointed to his cubby hole on the model, "wearing our Mae Wests — that's what we called our life-jackets — and trying to keep our heads down."

"I remember saying to Dan, 'Y'know the shore's not that far off mate. All we got to do it roll over the side and swim for it.'"

"Dan thought about this for a while, as the noise of firing seemed to get louder, with our own guns occasionally joining in."

Then he said: "Yeah, I'm with you, mate. Which side do you fancy....we've got hungry sharks over there, and mad fuzzy-wuzzies ashore this side, just waiting to cut your throat."

My Dad had been a faraway mystery man throughout most of my wartime childhood. And even when he came home, it was only now and again like this that I got a glimpse of his life as a fighting sailor — in some yarn of his that briefly pierced the fog of war.

"Not many matelots have been ordered to stand by to sink the flagship of the fleet," he casually mentioned one day.

It happened in the Battle of Narvik when the Germans over-ran Norway in April 1940. A force led by HMS Penelope, and including the destroyers Kimberley and Eskimo, were steaming up a fiord to join the attack on a force of German warships and transports.

"On this trip Penelope was regarded as a bit of a jinx ship," Dad said. "You know how superstitious sailors are. Well she lived up to her reputation that day all right. Halfway up the fiord, the bitch ran aground and ripped a slice out of her bottom."

Captain Yates thought he'd have to scuttle her to keep her out of German hands and ordered the crew to put on their Mae Wests and be ready to go over the side. Our destroyers were standing by to pick them up fast — don't forget we were practically in the Arctic.

"Kimberley was ordered to fire a torpedo into her as soon as the last man left....and since I was duty torpedo man, it would be my finger on the trigger. Imagine that — I could see that for the rest of my life I'd be known as the matelot that sank his own flagship!"

As it happened the chief engineer Commander Best managed to get one engine going and Penelope was able to limp to safety with the crew.

Just as well. My father-in-law Walter Ness, a Highland Scot from Oban, was a signals petty officer in HMS Penelope. Mind you, he never really took to Dad's yarn.

I was chatting to Dad once about a story I was reading where the hero, a sea officer in Nelson's time, struck lucky in the matter of prize money, retired ashore and set up his carriage in a country mansion in Hampshire. I mentioned it to my father saying something like, "Those were the days eh, Dad?"

"I had some prize money once," he said, "don't you remember? The admiralty sent me a cheque for a hundred quid. Well, that was my share of the loot from an Italian freighter we captured in the Med."

I didn't remember. So he told me the story of how sometime in 1941 they put a shot across the bows of an Italian freighter that promptly surrendered.

"She was carrying hundreds of Fiat cars for the Italian troops in North Africa," he said. "They must have fetched a pretty penny for me to get a hundred quid. Mind, I didn't get the money until years later, long after the war ended. Your uncles — dead jealous, o'course — said they reckoned all matelots were no better than pirates. But I notice they had no big objection to downing a few pints to celebrate my bit o' luck."

I mentioned the fog of war. Sometimes, of course, this fog was intentional, the Admiralty being keen to keep quiet about many things, such as ship losses and movements that could conceivably be of use to the enemy. In trying to trace my father's career recently I discovered that though ships' logs of the 1940s are now open in the national archives, the movements of humble lower deck ratings like my father are not always clear. My father died at the age of 80 in 1985 so I can't ask him.

For instance one story about HMS Kimberley only came to light a couple of years ago. Back in April 1941 as the Germans over-ran the Allied forces in Greece, the mayor of a small village and his 13-year-old son helped a group of five New Zealand soldiers to escape in a small boat. They were headed for Crete when they were picked up by Kimberley.

Some 63 years later the boy — now the famous Civil Rights lawyer George Bizos — was awarded the highest honour of the International Bar Association at their annual meeting in Auckland and took the opportunity to try to find relatives of the soldiers he and his father had helped in the war.

So it was that George who, after his rescue, became a South African and went on to defend Nelson Mandela during apartheid, met the families of those Kiwi soldiers in a tearful reunion in Auckland in 2004. George showed them photos taken by one of the crew, of the rescue at sea, the rail of the destroyer lined with sailors (one of whom was probably my father) and soldiers taken off as the Germans over-ran Greece.

I treasure the link that my Dad — who so nearly moved to South Africa in 1939 — was part of this adventure. In many ways he was years ahead of his time on what later came to be called self-determination. And how he'd have loved to tell that story.

Sailors (and soldiers evacuated from Greece) line the rail as
HMS Kimberley rescues 13-year-old George Bizos,
his father and New Zealand soldiers (1941)

Dad left HMS Kimberley later in 1941 and, after a spell ashore at HMS Canopus in Alexandria, he joined the cruiser HMS Naiad in December — about the time the Japanese attacked Pearl Harbor and brought the United States into the war.

Meanwhile things were getting tougher for the Royal Navy defending Malta and our supply lines in the Med, and the Eighth Army fighting Rommel's Afrika Korps in North Africa. The RAF fought hard, but they were desperately short of planes — and Rommel controlled the Libyan airfields.

In March, HMS Naiad and her escort force of destroyers under Philip Vian (later Admiral of the Fleet Sir Philip Vian) took a supply convoy to Malta. Early in the evening of March 11, Naiad was ambushed by a U-boat (U565) and sunk with a single torpedo with the loss of 82 sailors.

Three destroyers picked up the 585 survivors within half an hour.

Sir Philip, in his book Action This Day, graphically describes leaving Naiad with his signal officer Peter Hankey. They had to slither down the side of the doomed ship as she listed at an angle of 60 degrees. He was suffering from a large carbuncle on his bum and told Hankey he was dreading the slide over the barnacles encrusting the half of the hull normally under water. Hankey tried to cheer him up by saying the cold seawater "will probably do it the world of good."

Vian became celebrated as the navy's foremost fighting officer of World War II — Vian he was. Clearly, Vain he was not.

It was soon after this that Dad turned up on our doorstep, not exactly dripping wet but in a borrowed pongo uniform.

**********

Dad's long period of 'survey', including his treatment at Haslar, lasted until early 1943 when they drafted him to HMS Vectis, aka the Gloucester Hotel on the waterfront at Cowes. Typically, the navy interpreted 'light duties' literally, if not ironically. As a leading torpedo man, Dad would have been an electrician: the navy's electrical branch were originally torpedo men. So he was appointed as electrical maintenance man for the hotel, at this time known as a 'stone frigate' and fleet headquarters for the Isle of Wight.

It was a bit of a comedown for the old Gloucester which, in the heyday of yachting had rivalled the Royal Squadron as the place to rub shoulders with the 'Knights of the Solent' Sir Tommy Lipton, and Sir Tommy Sopwith, and other magnates who poured big bucks into trying to win the coveted America's Cup for their respective countries with their huge J-Class yachts.

Recently it was won by a team representing Switzerland — which might once have stretched Tommy Lipton's eyes — but, fair enough, their navy's probably bigger than ours now.

Cowes had been the place to be ever since Queen Victoria and Prince Albert took a shine to it and built a summer palace for themselves at Osborne House overlooking the Solent.

During the invasion scares, it was thought that the Luftwaffe would drop parachute troops onto the island (as they did in Crete) and use it as a jumping-off point for an overwhelming assault on England. Hadn't the Romans named the place Vectis? And didn't that mean 'lever' in Latin? Maybe they saw the place as the lever to crack open the defences of the mainland (well that's my theory). Fanciful, maybe. But the fact is that travel to and from the island was very restricted in wartime. My mother and I had to have 'passports' in order to visit Dad at Hotel HMS Vectis. This was a piece of card with our names and some official jargon, and a date stamp.

We made several trips over to Cowes, which we could see had been heavily bombed by the Luftwaffe in 1940 and 1941, the targets being the aircraft works and shipyards along the River Medina. Among the many heroes of that period the Free Polish navy stands out. One of their destroyers, the Blyskawica, had been to White's shipyard on the Medina for a refit and was anchored in the river during the Blitz. Night after night the Polish sailors gave the Luftwaffe a hot reception with their anti-aircraft fire. To this day anyone from Poland is pretty sure of a warm welcome to Cowes.

**********

When my father was finally invalided out of the navy in 1944 — only to find a nice sinecure job in Clarence Yard as a laboratory assistant — he and Mum moved out of the shared house in Peel Road to return to the now virtually re-built house which we were bombed out of in 1941 at 34 Elmhurst Road (later renumbered 56). Grannie and the uncles went back to Queen's Road and took over the house next door to the Queen's Hotel.

The change devastated me. I never got over the loss of the family — at least until the 1960s, by which time I had one of my own.

The up-side was that my father and I became closer. Later in life I realised he showed a surprising aptitude for handling a stroppy son. First, he persuaded me to join the navy cadets at HMS Victory in Portsmouth, I wasn't quite ten when I joined. With a handful of other Gosport kids I used to go over on the ferry after school two evenings a week, being careful to take the 3d subscription with me each time. You didn't want to upset the tough petty officers and senior ratings who ran the cadet 'ship' at the barracks in Queen Street, Portsea. They believed in 'keeping good order and discipline' with a sharp tongue and a swift backhander.

Often there were musters on Saturdays too: a trip to HMS Excellent, the gunnery school at Whale Island, to see the big guns (and the bear they kept as a mascot), or perhaps a cruise up the harbour, rowing or better still, sailing the whaler through the crowded anchorage, lined with dozens of warships.

We even had our own junior field gun crew. With a lighter, smaller gun, of course, but we went through the same routine as the tough guys who used to compete in the national tattoos —

Run up with the gun and ammunition limber....

Unlimber and remove wheels from gun carriage....

Set up rope bridges across a ravine....

Run up the parts of the gun, carriage, wheels and limber; haul them over the ravine....

Re-assemble the gun, limber up, load and fire a one-round salute....

All in less time than it takes to describe.

Our demo was in demand at wartime fêtes and fundraisers, along with our popular hornpipe display, complete with flashing blades of our cutlass drill. It was all satisfyingly warlike.

But best of all, for me, were the times we went to the rifle range. We had the use of a lighter .22 version of the Lee Enfield .303 rifle, the standard weapon for British forces in World War II.

I never discovered what the Royal Navy used the .22 for; there was a theory it was for shooting at floating enemy mines at sea to set them off well clear of the ship, but who knows? All I can say is that it was probably the most accurate weapon of the time over 25 yards. You had to be completely cack-handed or half-blind not to be able to get at least one bullseye in your five-rounds-rapid.

After the first painful weeks as recruits (maggots in our tatty civvy rags), we were sent to the navy's tailor's in Hay Street, off Queen Street, to be measured for a uniform — full square-rig with big collar and a navy blue carefully folded silk kerchief round the neck and smartly tied off at the front. We had bell-bottomed trousers, too. But unfortunately cadet uniform insisted on gaiters up to the knees. What a pain they were to lace up, and very uncomfortable to wear.

They had to be cleaned every time and treated with blanco which, wet or dry, would somehow get everywhere, smudging trousers, jumper, even your cap.

"Boy Bull — 'ave you been out in the snow? Get that birdshit off your uniform you filthy little gash bin," orders the veteran PO in charge of the parade.

It says it all about the popularity of the navy cadet force that we were prepared to put up with blanco-ed gaiters rather than miss cadet nights.

Eventually I gained my coveted proficiency badge which meant I had learned my knots and splices, and all the other priceless information in the Manual of Seamanship Part 1. In fact I stayed with the navy cadets for two years until the grammar school forced us to re-muster for their own B Company, Army Cadet Force. (With all that we had learned from the navy, we ex-matelot recruits sailed through the poor old Pongo's training programme — and I found, to my great delight, that this exempted me from a great deal of boring drill when I got called up for national service in the Royal Air Force at 21).

The navy also taught me a number of other useful skills, including hand-to-hand fighting (all the dirty moves, like punching well below the belt, head-butting and sticking a thumb in the other guy's eye). And I took, like a duck to water, to the navy's unique way of swearing. Make no mistake, our Bomb Alley Kids, having grown up in a seaport, were no strangers to the grammatical tenses and moods of every permutation of swear-word. For instance, what a revelation it was at the age of ten when it dawned on me that "Fookinewcassel," wasn't all one word.

But real navy cussing had an extra-creativity of its own:

'Enough to make an OD's missus cough up blood' (Something shocking)

'Enough to dry up the milk in a nun's tits' (Even more shocking)

'Get up out of my fucking chair you little spunk bubble' (To a junior)

'Awkward slab-sided, Dutch-built bugger' (To a foreign sailor)

'Useless grass-combing, sod-bustin' bastard' (A landsman).

The restoration of discipline as we boys joined the navy cadets and the longer-serving Dads were released from the forces, or given home postings, spelt the end of the easy freedom of the Bomb Alley Kids.

On the other hand, among the consolations was the arrival of the Yanks early in 1944. Older sisters and even some of the younger mothers thought so, too. Here were guys looking and talking just like the stars in the movies. They wore neatly pressed khaki uniforms, and even the GIs had superior peaked caps and neatly-tailored tunics. We never saw them in boots, only smart shoes with shiny toecaps.

We kids quickly learnt to call out, "Got any gum, chum?" by way of greeting. And we nearly always got a handful of what they called 'candy,' of which they seemed to have an inexhaustible supply. They had access to sheer nylon stockings, too, which rendered them irresistible to the girls (I nearly wrote 'virtually irresistible' — but virtue really had nothing to do with it.).

Our gang had Yanks at close quarters since the Toc H club at Bourton House became a local version of a Stage Door Canteen for relaxing GIs, with jitterbugging every night on the dancefloor — and jig-a-jigging on warm nights amid the trees and shrubs of the extensive gardens, to judge by the dozens of condoms littering the drive to much sniggering amusement for us streetwise kids.

Visiting my Grannie one day, I found her in the front garden chatting to two GIs.

"How polite and charming these doughboys are," she says after they moved on.

"Why d'ye call them that, Grannie?"

"Doughboys? That's what we called them when they came over in the last war," she explains. "Could have been these lads' fathers."

"Most people call 'em Yanks, or GIs."

"I don't suppose it matters what we call them," she says. "It's a comfort to have them on our side. They're more like us than the Frogs, say, or anybody else come to that. And they have such nice manners. That's part of their charm. It's no wonder the girls like them — they do know how to treat a lady."

I'm a bit surprised by all this. It took a lot to win over my Grannie — she was nobody's fool. If she said Yanks were OK, then I was happy to hear it. Me and the rest of the gang certainly found them easy to get along with. I suppose there were plenty of Brits who resented them, especially the young men, but on the whole most people in Gosport sided with Grannie.

Our gang used to meet our new heroes at the swimming baths. We'd hang around them on the terraces, helping them eat their candy, and explaining the unfathomable mysteries of life 'over here.'

We taught them songs like:

"Eye-tiddley eye-ty, carry me back to Blighty

Blighty is the place for me."

They countered with Johnny Mercer's:

"Mairzy doats and dozy doats and liddle lamzy divey

A kiddley divey too, wouldn't you?"

We swapped comics, too. They'd hoot with glee over the antics of Desperate Dan and Lord Snooty....and were politely respectful of heroes like Rockfist Rogan, RAF, in the Champion.

We treasured the American comics they handed out and worshipped Superman or Dick Tracey. Enterprising lad that I was, I found a coupon in one of these that promised luminous logos to sew on your shirt:

"Please rush me my favourite Glo Crests (tick box under illustration). Mail ten cents for each Glo Crest and ten cents handling/delivery to...." I reckoned a shilling each would cover it, so I filled in the form and sent it in an envelope with a two-bob bit (two shillings, nowadays 10p) to the Chicago address.

To my delight, a month later my Glo Crests of Captain Marvel and Superman duly arrived. Far too precious to be put on a shirt, I fixed them up on the mantelpiece of my bedroom, where I watched them glow every night for at least a year.

Our friendly Yanks often used to exchange names and addresses with us, especially if they had met our families. At the time I didn't really understand why, I imagine that I just put it down to a kind of politeness; that's the way they were — wanting people to like them, to understand them.

The Yanks came to Gosport, of course, because this was a jumping-off area for the invasion of Normandy. Large sections of the Mulberry Harbour were built in yards around the town and towed across to make an instant harbour to supply the Allied troops. After a while us kids became aware that many of those young Americans did not survive D-Day, or the march on Berlin.

But it wasn't until years later that I finally realised why the GIs were so keen to swap names and addresses. It was so that if they did not return from the war, their folks back in Chicago or North Carolina might be able to write to a family in Gosport and know that their son didn't simply cross the Atlantic to die; but made a mark in life, met and had fun with some of the kids, some of the people that he'd died for. I for one am truly thankful for the sacrifice.

**********

It wasn't the only contact we Bomb Alley Kids had with foreign troops. As the German armies began to crumble under the double onslaught of the Russians from the east and the Americans and British in the west, huge numbers of prisoners of war began to pile up. Many of these were shipped back to England, and Gosport was one of the places where a prisoner-of-war camp was established.

This was sited in an area of open land behind the Royal Navy training establishment at HMS St Vincent, next to Forton Lake. The prisoners were shipped in via the railway from Fareham, arriving at the bombed-out Gosport station in Spring Garden Lane.

When word of this reached Jono, he alerted the gang. "There's 'undreds of Jerry prisoners arriving at the railway station," he told us. "and we're going to give the dirty bastards a special welcome."

The plan was for us to arm ourselves with our catapults and plenty of stones and bricks and take them to the 'ladder' — the bridge over the railway at the top of Queen's Road. Then, as the prisoners passed underneath in open 'cattle' trucks, we would open fire on them.

So off we went, up the ladder and onto the bridge. It was a favourite place to stand and wait for a train to come through; we loved to stand in the clouds of steam vapour as the puffing engine trundled past below. Sometimes a burst of actual steam scorched your leg (we wore short trousers remember), but we reckoned it was worth risking for the thrill.

So here we are leaning on the rail of the bridge looking down on the station off to our right.

"Be like shootin' fish in a barrel," says Dave, who tends to be like that.

"Yeah we'll give those Jerry bastards something to remember us by," goes Big Jono, taking a practice aim at the rails with his catapult. We pile up stocks of brick and stone missiles from the nearest bommie so as to have ammo ready at hand.

We don't have long to wait. We can hear the train coming down the track from Fareham well before we see it. The driver gives a toot on the whistle as his loco passes the piggeries, and here it comes, a line of open trucks behind the engine, slowing to a walking pace around the bend by St Vincent sports field. I'm excited; we're really going into battle, though I'm a bit nervous — who wouldn't be — at the thought of facing up to the Wehrmacht.

I can see a crowd of men in grey uniforms, some with greatcoats on, mostly sitting in the bottom of the trucks. I'm getting ready to lob a brick down on the first square-head I see. The engine passes underneath enveloping us in the usual cloud of vapour.

"Wait for the word and all fire together," commands Jono. But the word never comes.

Somehow first sight of the enemy is a bit of shock. This bunch are wearing field-grey all right, but they are not the smart, arrogant storm troopers we've seen at the pictures.

Below us, as the trucks roll slowly into the station, we are looking at a ragged bunch of....well, they look like kids. These prisoners are not much older than us. Like the Yanks, they could be our older brothers or cousins. They look cold, most of them, and miserable — then one of them, looking up, waves uncertainly at us.

Suddenly I'm ashamed and drop my brick on the bridge. Jono stuffs his catapult out of sight. We stand silently watching as the trucks reach the platform and a group of armed Royal Marines, bayonets fixed, fan out and shepherd the Germans into line, ready to march them to the camp.

Nobody says much as we shuffle off back down Queen's Road to our bommie. They all feel like I do, I guess. Jono and Dave start a fire going in a half-hearted sort of way. The whole thing has been a bit of a let-down, and nobody's particularly happy about it.

"It's Saturday — I'm going home to get my pocket-money," says Les. Not a bad idea, I could go and get mine, I think. Jono suddenly jumps to his feet.

"I know what we'll do. S'pose we put our money together and buy some chocolate for those poor bastards in the cattle trucks. Hey, what about it?"

Well this was a bit of a choker, and you can tell some of the others think so, too. But Dave and Les seem to think it's a good idea. Might make us feel better.

"I don't want to give them losers any of my sweets," — that's Bobby, one of the snotty-nosed little kids dumped on us to look after. A swift clip round the ear from Dave brings him to his senses.

So, in the afternoon, when the next train came in, the gang was back on the ladder, well-stocked up with ammo (thanks to the kind co-operation of Mrs Munday and Mrs Moss at the sweet shops in Queen's Road). And when the train crawled past — we let 'em have it with bars of chocolate and Mars bars. And I hope the buggers were suitably grateful.

Above Left – In the finest traditions of the service – me in my Royal Navy cadet square-rig. My right arm is strangely skewed to show off the proficiency badge I've just won.

Above Right – Cousin Peter and his little brother Winston pictured at the end of the war.

Winston asks: "Now it's over, will it be good again like before the war?"

Peter says: "It may take a while, but one day it will be better than ever."

# Chapter Eleven
## Madness on a May Night

Although there had been a lot of talk about it, the end of the war came rather suddenly down our way. I was hanging about the street with the other kids after school as usual, when someone listening to the BBC shouted out of the window: "It's all over."

We scooted straight home. And as I ran up the back garden path my Mum, quick on the uptake as always, struggled with the blackout fitting and threw open the new French windows. It brought me up sharp. They had been blasted to bits in 1941 and replaced in 1944, but they hadn't actually been opened since the blackout began in 1939. This was therefore a truly momentous thing.

"S'over, Mum," I shouted. "I know," she said, hugging me to her, the unstoppable tears running down her face. Then she moved the ironing board out of the way, and made me kneel down with her.

"Thank you, Lord," she said.

She'd waited nearly six years for that. And I realised that I would never again end my bedtime prayers as I had most of my life, by "Please-God-let-the-war-be-over-soon."

Then we sat down and looked at each other. It meant: what happens next? After so long, this was going to leave a bit of a gap.

**********

What actually happened next was VE Night.

179

My father came home from his job in Clarence Yard and we went to join the rest of our family at Auntie Gert's house. Then, led by my pretty female cousins and their friends, we all went to a dance. I'm not sure where it was held, but there were a lot of airmen there, so it was probably Grange airfield.

The girls showed us a short cut, along a path by neighbours' gardens, down a narrow lane, overhung with thick may blossom, over a ditch, to emerge by a side gate in a barbed wire fence. The gate had been left unlocked, as the girls well knew. My aunt frowned: how long had this been going on?

The club or mess must have been hoarding its beer rations for weeks because there was no shortage of drinks. The fathers soon had pints in front of them, Mum and Auntie sipped wine cocktails; Green Goddess, I remember was a favourite. The girls and their pals went straight for gin and Italian vermouth — known as a gin and It.

Some of the older lads, armed with brown ale and Gold Flake cigarettes, swaggered about as gauche young men will, trying to look glum and moaning that it had all ended before they could 'get into the show.' Uncle Jim, who was doing his bit as an Army sergeant, said nothing. The mothers looked rather pleased.

Someone proposed a toast to Uncle Charlie, a sergeant in the Hampshires captured at Dunkirk along with Uncle Jim's two brothers Len and Bob, who were both in the Green Jackets. All three were now waiting somewhere in defeated Germany to come home. Other families at nearby tables joined in, and pretty soon everyone was toasting everyone else.

Uncle Jim, not normally a speechmaker, suddenly stood up and called on people to raise their glasses to 'The

Home Front' along with some remarks about the women left behind, their sense of duty, and so on. It got quite a cheer.

Cousin Peter, a few years older than me, led me outside where it was still light (thanks to the magic of Double British Summer Time) and we prowled about, first looking for birds' eggs and then, as freedom dawned on us, we took a look at whatever military hardware was lying about. I vaguely recall playing happily with an anti-aircraft gun.

Peter suddenly grabbed my arm: "Look!"

I saw that suddenly there were bonfires glowing all over the place. Imagine, bonfires. I don't think I'd ever seen one at night before, apart from those arranged by the Luftwaffe of course.

When we crept back into the dancehall, no-one took the slightest notice. For once no-one cared about us. The pretty cousins, in pale, shiny dresses (made, I suspect, from parachute silk) were jitterbugging with the airmen to a brassy swing band.

The noise was deafening. I suddenly spotted Mum and Auntie Gert. They were dancing on top of a table, lifting their skirts and showing their knickers (also made from parachute silk). What's more, my Dad and Uncle Jim were cheering them on.

Peter and I couldn't believe it. What was happening to these people?

"Better take ourselves home," he said. So we trailed back down the lane, back to the house, where the toddlers were abed and the grandparents were listening to the wireless.

We were drinking our cocoa when the casualties started coming in.

First Jean, cousin Jimmy's girlfriend. The girls put her on the sofa, where she lay with her eyes tight shut, gently moaning, "Jimmy? Where are you, Jimmy?"

The girls turned out the lights and made Peter sit by her holding her hand. "Here's Jimmy," they said, and rushed off back to the party.

Peter comforted her until she fell asleep. "It's okay, darling, I'm here," he kept saying in the deepest voice he could manage.

The mothers were next, half-carried in by neighbours and put straight to bed.

Then the fathers. Covered in mud where they had tried to take the short cut. Accompanied, unaccountably, by a young Canadian airman. They stood swaying and grinning. Uncle Jim looked at his watch. "Be more bones made than broken tonight," he said, then he remembered us and ordered us to bed.

"Worst night of the bloody war," said Peter, as we turned in.

**********

The party mood ushered in a new era. We still had unfinished business with the Japs in the Pacific, and there were still plenty of servicemen still at war. But, ugly though the fighting was out there, change at home was the biggest concern. There was a consensus among returning servicemen that 'never again were the old top-hatted gang of privileged parasites' to be allowed to push the rest of us around.

The 1945 election was looming; many servicemen were planning to stand as candidates. Anyone with any savvy at all could see that Clement Atlee's Labour party had the backing of the majority of men returning to civvy street. And that was the mood of the women, too. Though — and here was a case in point — only those over 30 were able to vote anyway. That was one of the wrongs that was going to be put right.

Everyone agreed that Churchill had been a great war leader, but gratitude has its limits. And the majority of voters said : "Sorry, Winston, we don't want you as prime minister right now." That thank-you came later — after the social revolution was firmly in place.

Gosport continued to vote Tory, as it has done ever since, on the ground that the Tories were more likely to keep the Royal Navy, its dockyards, victualling, ammunition, and aircraft repair yards, the great milch cow that provided jobs for Gosport people. But there was still a feeling that change had to come.

The Bomb Alley Kids realised their day was done. We were headed for secondary education. So 1945 was to be our last summer of fun before more serious living was lined up for us. We had two things to do.

One was our first proper football match. At Newtown School we'd had no football throughout the war — probably because our teachers were not up to it. The school mascot, an old-fashioned teddy bear in a red-and-white striped football shirt, had been lined up next to a glass case holding some ancient silver trophies, under the venerable school honours board in the hall. But he hadn't seen a game since 1939. The best we'd been able to do, apart from kicking a tennis ball about in the playground, was occasionally punting about an old leather ball stuffed with paper instead of a properly inflated bladder.

But when challenged to a Victory celebration game by Leesland School, we could not refuse. So Jono and the gang took it upon ourselves to get up a team. Apart from the five of us, we recruited another six from the top class — including the agile Morrie Newnham, who always played in goal in our knockabouts and Biffer Owen as centre forward, incidentally a son of the Ivy, the war widow mentioned earlier.

We practised a bit with a borrowed ball in Walpole Park, trying out shots at goal, which Morrie mostly stopped, and a bit of practice dribbling and tackling. We decided that our best bet was to rely on natural talent.

Leesland were posh enough to have a sports master and he organised the borrowing of a pitch in Gordon Park, on the opposite side of Daisy Lane from their school. The game was fixed for a Saturday morning.

I don't recall whether any of our parents or teachers came — I would be very surprised if they did. We each had a football shirt, but not all of them were the same colours — and only two or three were in red and white. Some of our team had managed to get football boots, probably borrowed from older brothers. Leesland, of course, were all in school colours, though not all of them had proper boots either.

The ref — a teacher borrowed from some neutral school — blew his whistle, Jono booted the ball forward and the full Newtown team charged after it. As a shock tactic it worked like a dream. We rushed the ball down to Leesland's penalty area, with the overwhelmed enemy floundering along behind. Then Jono booted the ball clean over the crossbar.

This set a pattern for the game. Whenever one of us got the ball, the entire team, except goalie Morrie, rushed with it at the defenders. But whenever it rolled loose, or was booted too far ahead, we lost it. We had no notion of passing the ball — but Leesland had, and they quickly found out that all they had to do was tap the ball to and fro between them. For a while we managed to hold them out by sheer brute strength. But inevitably, our lack of skill in front of goal let us down.

Our defence tactic was the same. Leesland would tap the ball between them and move gradually down the pitch. We continued to rush about after the ball. When one of the attacking forwards hung onto it too long, one (or more) of us would charge smack into him and regain possession....until the ref started to notice and began to issue free kicks.

The result was inevitable — they could score, we could not. At half-time we were one down. By the second half, we were tired and moved more and more slowly, still in a mob. Their centre-forward banged in a hat-trick. We lost 4-0 and it would have been a lot worse without Morrie between the sticks.

I'm convinced that no-one feels shame like a kid from the back streets. 'Face' was all-important to the Bomb Alley boys. For us there was nowhere to hide. Gosport was a small town and we met Leeslanders everywhere we went. On top of that we were all due to change schools in September — to move up into the senior schools: Clarence Square for most of the Newtowners — unless they were clever enough to pass the ball for the County (Grammar) School, or for the Central School for craftsmen, engineers or apprentices.

Who wanted to move to another school with a reputation as a loser? The skies were never sunny that summer. Even the promise of getting our beaches at

Stokes Bay back (when all the barbed wire, tank traps and underwater mines had been removed) couldn't wipe out the stain.

**********

August came. Preparations for the Gosport Victory Carnival began. Jono's dad tried to interest him in the Grand Soap-Box Derby billed as one of the main events of the show.

"Just the thing for you lot," he told us as we mooched about in his garden. "You've always made pretty good trollies right?" We winced at 'trollies.' Nobody called 'em that. Every gang had one to mess about with — and it was our 'cart' not 'trolley.'

We weren't interested, until he showed up with the posh pram wheels. They were twice the diameter of ordinary wheels. And they came complete with well-oiled axles. Idly Dave and Les gave the wheels a spin.

"Not bad are they?" said Jono's dad. "I've got a couple of nice pieces of timber for the frame that you can have. All you need is a decent box to mount on it."

"Where'd you get them wheels, Dad?"

"Never you mind that," he said, laying a forefinger alongside his nose and giving us a knowing look.

Well, a nod was as good as a wink to a blind horse, and the gang knew when to stay shtum. We set to work, half-heartedly perhaps at first, but then with growing enthusiasm as the strongest, highest soap-box cart ever began to take shape. The rear axle was fixed to a hefty piece of oak before being bolted to the box. The mobile front axle was fitted with a strong lock-nutted bolt, and the steering cord wasn't cord at all but a piece of cable liberated from the back yard of the Radio Rentals shop in Jamaica Place.

And when we finished painting it a patriotic red, white and blue, compared with anything we'd had before, it was the Rolls Royce of soap-box carts. We got an old tarpaulin to cover it from prying rivals — word was that every gang in town was going to enter the Soap-Box Derby.

We practised racing it around the navy's St Vincent field. There were six of us in the team, in three pairs. The race would be over a mile, four times round a 440-yard circular course. A team of two for each cart — one pushing and one steering — with a changeover after each circuit.

Our three pairs were trained up so that we had two replacements for our lead racers — Jono and Dave — and another spare team just in case.

We practised pushing and steering by the hour. We ran back and forth around St Vincent field — and then even faster when the duty instructors came to chase us out. And every evening we fiddled about with the wheels, the axles, oiling and adjusting to squeeze the last ounce of speed out of her. We named her Queen's Roller and painted it neatly on the back.

On Carnival Day we paraded her down Stoke Road to St George's Barracks field and pushed her over to where the others were lined up.

"Blimey," said Jono. "Look at 'em."

It was bit of a shock. There were six other gleaming Soap-Box Carts neatly parked up near the start line. One, entered by a Scout troop, seemed twice as high off the ground as ours. Then there was the all-black Hardway Kinger, a streamlined, metallic monster.

The boys standing guard over their carts seemed twice as big as normal boys. Athletes every one.

"'Ere we go again," said Dave. Just how I felt.

Jono looked at him.

"You droppin' out?"

"Course not. Jus'...well, look at 'em!"

The Derby marshal came over and started going over the rules. Us reserve drivers and riders were herded back to watch the race from the compound, and the carts, led by the awesome Kinger, were pushed onto the starting grid. There was Jono with arms stretched out, hands firmly gripping the edges of the soap box, Dave sitting up, trying to be as light as a feather, with the steering cable in his hands.

The marshal fired a Very pistol signal flare and the crews rushed forward. We suddenly became aware of how big the watching crowd was. Hundreds had turned out to see the race.

At the end of the first circuit, the Scouts were ahead, Hardway close behind. Then Dave was leaping from the cart and Jono was scrabbling aboard....off they went. The rest of us were jumping up and down, yelling our heads off.

Hardway snatched the lead in the second leg, and Dave managed to move up the pecking order.

In the third leg, stamina began to tell. Jono, going like a train, moved into the lead. Then Dave leapt out and Jono grabbed the reins in a lightning changover. They pelted off, the rest of the gang screaming at them "Faster....faster....faster." The crowd were on their feet screaming with excitement.

Over the line they went, a clear two lengths in front. Dave and Jono collapsed on the grass, utterly blown. the rest of the gang rushed over and danced around them.

The Mayor came up to hand over a huge silver cup. We had our pictures taken with Jono and Dave holding it up between them. We'd done it. The Queen's Road mob — best gang in Gosport. Official.

"Feels like we won the war, boys," said Jono.

In Churchill's words — it was our finest hour.

\*\*\*\*\*\*\*\*\*\*

## Postscript

Remember Ivy Owen, Gosport's first war widow? She later remarried, became Mrs Greenaway and had another son.

I saw her yesterday. She still lives in that same house in Strathmore Road that she watched them build before she moved in as a young bride. She lost her first husband Bernard, a Fleet Air Arm flyer, when the carrier HMS Courageous was sunk in September 1939.

But, you know, she saw them all come and go....Hitler, Mussolini, Stalin, Franco....yes, and Roosevelt and even Churchill. And she's still here.

She still looks after herself and every day, unless it's blowing a gale, she walks down to Walpole Park to feed the geese and swans as she has done for more years than anyone can count.

I said to her: "Hello Mrs Greenaway....you must be about 104."

"How dare you," she said with a wicked grin, " I'm only 103."

Young Ivy Bell, the war widow who outlived them all....now 103